DATE DUE

AP 7 '99			
JE 3 '00			
OC 16 '00			
MR 9 '01			
MY 23 '01			
DE 7 '02			
MY 23 '07			

DEMCO 38-296

Jordan I. Kosberg, PhD
Juanita L. Garcia, EdD
Editors

Elder Abuse: International and Cross-Cultural Perspectives

Pre-publication
REVIEWS,
COMMENTARIES,
EVALUATIONS . . .

"This book is an informative, global glimpse of the growing field of elder abuse. It provides a good complement to other emerging literature on aging from the fields of comparative social policy, cultural studies, human development, and social treatment. Specific chapters written by experts from ten different countries, as well as an overview and a synthesis at the end by the editors give this book genuine depth."

Sharon M. Keigher, PhD
Associate Professor and Director,
Social Work Programs School
of Social Welfare, University
of Wisconsin-Milwaukee

"**T**he problem of elder abuse, as documented in this book, is not limited to only one type of society or geographic area. Through this collection of ten chapters, the magnitude of the problem is vividly depicted as it occurs in both industrialized and nonindustrialized countries in all parts of the world. By examining the ways in which other countries are beginning to deal with the problem, this book is an important resource in deepening our understanding of elder abuse and the problems needed to combat it. "

Carole Cox, DSW
Associate Professor
School of Social Services
The Catholic University
of America

"**T**his book is a fascinating portrayal of the wide ranging differences across the globe in awareness as well as action concerning the growing problem of elder abuse and neglect. Variations in population aging as well as social, cultural, and economic characteristics are highlighted–such as changes in migration patterns, roles of women, availability of social insurance, and even attitudes toward older people.

Practitioners, educators and researchers alike would find this book enlightening, especially those in the field of health, mental health, and aging."

Connie Saltz, PhD, MSW
Associate Professor
School of Social Work
University of Maryland
at Baltimore

"**T**his book deals with a phenomenon, elder abuse, that has been recognized as a social problem only since the late 1970s or early 1980s and, essentially, only in certain parts of the world. Through their own informative and lucid introductory and concluding chapters on elder abuse and edited contributions from knowledgeable authors in ten different Western and non-Western societies, Kosberg and Garcia have opened our eyes to its worldwide presence and significance."

Wiley P. Mangum, PhD
Associate Professor
of Gerontology
and Interim Chair,
Department of Geronotology, University of South Florida, Tampa

"**J**ordan Kosberg and Juanita Garcia have offered us a superb book. It is a remarkably comprehensive portrayal of the variety of approaches to defining, assessing and determining the prevalence of elder abuse, as well as the diversity of causes for abuse and their solutions.

A strength of this volume is the adherence by authors to an assigned format: the definition of elder abuse in the country; the extent of the problem; causes of the problem; societal attitudes regarding the existence of the problem; private and public efforts to prevent, detect and intervene in the problem; and policies to counteract the problem."

Sheldon S. Tobin, PhD
Professor, School of Social
Welfare and Research Associate,
University of Albany, SUNY

The Haworth Press, Inc.

Elder Abuse:
International and Cross-Cultural
Perspectives

Elder Abuse: International and Cross-Cultural Perspectives

Jordan I. Kosberg, PhD
Juanita L. Garcia, EdD
Editors

The Haworth Press, Inc.
New York · London

Elder Abuse: International and Cross-Cultural Perspectives has also been published as *Journal of Elder Abuse & Neglect*, Volume 6, Numbers 3/4 1995.

The development, preparation, and publication of this work has been undertaken with great care. However, the publisher, employees, editors, and agents of The Haworth Press and all imprints of The Haworth Press, Inc., including the Haworth Medical Press and Pharmaceutical Products Press, are not responsible for any errors contained herein or for consequences that may ensue from use of materials or information contained in this work. Opinions expressed by the author(s) are not necessarily those of The Haworth Press, Inc.

The Haworth Press, Inc., 10 Alice Street, Binghamton, NY 13904-1580 USA

Library of Congress Cataloging-in-Publication Data

Elder abuse: international and cross-cultural perspectives / Jordan I. Kosberg, Juanita L. Garcia, editors.
     p. cm.
Includes bibliographical references and index.
ISBN 1-56024-711-8 (alk. paper)
     1. Aged–Abuse of–Cross-cultural studies. 2. Aged–Crimes against–Cross-cultural studies.
     I. Kosberg, Jordan I., 1939- . II. Garcia, Juanita L.
HV6626.3.E435 1995   95-13449
362.6–dc20   CIP

INDEXING & ABSTRACTING

Contributions to this publication are selectively indexed or abstracted in print, electronic, online, or CD-ROM version(s) of the reference tools and information services listed below. This list is current as of the copyright date of this publication. See the end of this section for additional notes.

- *Abstracts in Social Gerontology: Current Literature on Aging,* National Council on the Aging, Library, 409 Third Street SW, 2nd Floor, Washington, DC 20024

- *Ageline Database,* American Association of Retired Persons, 601 E Street, NW, Washington, DC 20049

- *Behavioral Medicine Abstracts,* The Society of Behavioral Medicine, 103 South Adams Street, Rockville, MD 20850

- *Brown University Geriatric Research Application Digest "Abstracts Section,"* Brown University, Center for Gerontology & Health Care Research, c/o Box G-1B235, Providence, RI 02912

- *Cambridge Scientific Abstracts, Risk Abstracts,* Cambridge Information Group, 7200 Wisconsin Avenue #601, Bethesda, MD 20814

- *Caredata CD: The Social and Community Care Database,* National Institute for Social Work, 5 Tavistock Place, London WC1H 9SS, England

- *Communication Abstracts,* Temple University, 303 Annenberg Hall, Philadelphia, PA 19122

- *Criminal Justice Abstracts,* Willow Tree Press, 15 Washington Street, 4th Floor, Newark, NJ 07102

- *Criminal Justice Periodical Index,* University Microfilms, Inc., 300 North Zeeb Road, Ann Arbor, MI 48106

(continued)

- *Current Contents: Clinical Medicine/Life Sciences (CC:CM/LS) (Weekly Table of Contents Service), and Social Science Citation Index. Articles also Searchable Through Social SciSearch, ISI's Online Database and in ISI's Research Alert Current Awareness Service,* Institute for Scientific Information, 3501 Market Street, Philadelphia, PA 19104-3302 (USA)

- *Family Violence & Sexual Assault Bulletin,* Family Violence & Sexual Assault Institute, 1310 Clinic Drive, Tyler, TX 75701

- *Human Resources Abstracts (HRA),* Sage Publications, Inc., 2455 Teller Road, Newbury Park, CA 91320

- *Index to Periodical Articles Related to Law,* University of Texas, 727 East 26th Street, Austin, TX 78705

- *Inventory of Marriage and Family Literature (online and hard copy),* National Council on Family Relations, 3989 Central Avenue NE, Suite 550, Minneapolis, MN 55421

- *Mental Health Abstracts (online through DIALOG),* IFI/Plenum Data Company, 3202 Kirkwood Highway, Wilmington, DE 19808

- *Social Planning/Policy & Development Abstracts (SOPODA),* Sociological Abstracts, Inc., P. O. Box 22206, San Diego, CA 92192-0206

- *Social Work Abstracts,* National Association of Social Workers, 750 First Street NW, 8th Floor, Washington, DC 20002

- *Sociological Abstracts (SA),* Sociological Abstracts, Inc., P. O. Box 22206, San Diego, CA 92192-0206

- *Violence and Abuse Abstracts: A Review of Current Literature on Interpersonal Violence (VAA),* Sage Publications, Inc., 2455 Teller Road, Newbury, Park, CA 91320

(continued)

SPECIAL BIBLIOGRAPHIC NOTES

related to special journal issues (separates)
and indexing/abstracting

☐ indexing/abstracting services in this list will also cover material in any "separate" that is co-published simultaneously with Haworth's special thematic journal issue or DocuSerial. Indexing/abstracting usually covers material at the article/chapter level.

☐ monographic co-editions are intended for either non-subscribers or libraries which intend to purchase a second copy for their circulating collections.

☐ monographic co-editions are reported to all jobbers/wholesalers/approval plans. The source journal is listed as the "series" to assist the prevention of duplicate purchasing in the same manner utilized for books-in-series.

☐ to facilitate user/access services all indexing/abstracting services are encouraged to utilize the co-indexing entry note indicated at the bottom of the first page of each article/chapter/contribution.

☐ this is intended to assist a library user of any reference tool (whether print, electronic, online, or CD-ROM) to locate the monographic version if the library has purchased this version but not a subscription to the source journal.

☐ individual articles/chapters in any Haworth publication are also available through the Haworth Document Delivery Services (HDDS).

This book is dedicated to

Helen Duran Juarez
and
Alex Michael Sanchez

Wishing you long lives filled with health and happiness

ABOUT THE EDITORS

Jordan I. Kosberg, PhD, is Philip S. Fisher Professor and Director of The Centre for Applied Family Studies in the School of Social Work at McGill University in Montreal, Quebec. A gerontological social worker, he has been involved in research, training, and lecturing in the area of elder abuse and maltreatment since 1978. He has authored many articles on the topic of elder abuse and developed the Cost of Care Index (to screen potential family caregivers) and the High Risk Assessment Form (to identify older persons who are at high risk of abuse). Dr. Kosberg is a former member of the board of the National Committee for the Prevention of Elder Abuse and of the Florida Attorney General Task Force on Crime and the Elderly. He served on a national task force to establish a research agenda for elder abuse in the U.S. and Chaired a U.S. Attorney General Task Force on Elder Abuse.

Juanita L. Garcia, EdD, is Associate Professor in the Department of Gerontology at the University of South Florida. A psychologist, she has carried out research on culturally-diverse groups of elderly in the U.S. and on elderly women. She has lectured on elder abuse, chaired workshops and symposia on Hispanic elderly, and written on the psychological dimensions of caregiving stress leading to abuse and maltreatment. Dr. Garcia teaches courses on minority group elderly, and both she and Dr. Kosberg have lectured and presented papers world-wide.

Elder Abuse: International and Cross-Cultural Perspectives

CONTENTS

ALL HAWORTH BOOKS AND JOURNALS
ARE PRINTED ON CERTIFIED
ACID-FREE PAPER

Chapter 1

Introduction to the Book

Jordan I. Kosberg, PhD
Juanita L. Garcia, EdD

BACKGROUND

During the late 1960s and early 1970s, the identification of elder abuse was slowly gaining attention. Among the first printed accounts of abuse was an article on *"granny bashing"* in Great Britain (Burston, 1975). In the United States, causes of the abuse of an estimated 500,000 to 2,500,000 elderly persons each year were being discussed (U.S. Congress, 1980). A variety of theories and explanations for elder abuse were proposed (Kosberg, 1983; Phillips, 1986): sociological, psychological, economic, deviant behavior, intergenerational, social exchange, social ecological, among others. Researchers and practitioners (Kosberg, 1988; Quinn & Tomita, 1986) attempted to identify predictive variables for abusive behavior and high risk factors for the elderly, their caregivers, and family systems. Both antecedents to and consequences from types of abuse were investigated. Throughout the 1980s, increasing numbers of books, monographs, workshops, legislation, education, and

Jordan I. Kosberg is Philip Fisher Professor, School of Social Work, McGill University, Montreal, Quebec H3A 2A7. Juanita L. Garcia is Psychologist, Department of Gerontology, College of Arts and Sciences, University of South Florida.

[Haworth co-indexing entry note]: "Introduction to the Book." Kosberg, Jordan I., and Juanita L. Garcia. Co-published simultaneously in the *Journal of Elder Abuse & Neglect* (The Haworth Press, Inc.) Vol. 6, No. 3/4, 1995, pp. 1-12; and: *Elder Abuse: International and Cross-Cultural Perspectives* (ed: Jordan I. Kosberg and Juanita L. Garcia) The Haworth Press, Inc., 1995, pp. 1-12. Multiple copies of this article/chapter may be purchased from The Haworth Document Delivery Center [1-800-3-HA-WORTH; 9:00 a.m. - 5:00 p.m. (EST)].

1

research were undertaken on elder abuse. The activities continue today.

It has been generally believed that elder abuse was basically an American phenomenon inherent in its values and history. For example, following a Workshop on Violence sponsored by the U.S. Surgeon General in 1985, Kosberg (1986) testified before a U.S. Senate committee that elder abuse would not disappear until two dominant characteristics of American society disappeared: ageism and violence.

Beyond America, there was a belief that elder abuse was a problem in mainly, if not only, industrialized, westernized, and developed nations (U.S., Canada, Great Britain), for it was from these countries that literature on the topic of elder abuse emanated. One might have concluded that elder abuse was not a problem anywhere else in the world. Indeed, in international travels and conversations with those from other countries, one would have concluded that "there is no such problem here."

On a lecture and consulting trip to Australia in 1986, a co-editor of this book was asked not to speak on the topic of elder abuse because he was informed that it was not a problem. Yet, a group of social workers in one Australian city told him that elder abuse was very much a problem; a special issue of the *Australian Journal of Gerontology* (1993) on elder abuse and the chapter in this book have confirmed this declaration made several years earlier. In the same vein, at an international conference on aging, in 1987, a French woman confided to the co-editor, "Well, if elder abuse is a problem in France, we don't like to talk about it in public." German and Dutch professors admitted that they would be reluctant to talk about elder abuse in their countries with those from other countries. One said: "You Americans go overboard on too many things–physical fitness, smoking bans, and abusive behavior in the family."

Growing Awareness of Elder Abuse

In 1986 at a conference in Taiwan, the co-editor was approached by a social worker from Hong Kong who had just finished writing a report based upon his master's thesis and wished to pass on a copy of his study. His report was on elder abuse in Hong Kong (Chan, 1985). The study conducted under the supervision of two highly respected social gerontologists in Hong Kong, Dr. Alex Kwan and Dr. Nelson Chow, underscored the fact that elder abuse could exist in a country–an area of the world–where filial piety was said to be a sure deterrent to such adversities for older persons.

About this same period of time, a paper on elder abuse in Norway (Johns, Hydle, & Aschjem, 1987), co-authored by a Norwegian anthropologist, a geriatrician, and a psychiatric nurse, was presented at a conference in the U.S.; a book (written by a Japanese physician) was published on elder abuse in Japan (Kaneko, 1987); and a paper was written on a study of elder abuse in Denmark and Sweden (Tornstam, 1987). Thus, it is evident that elder abuse is a worldwide phenomenon, not limited to any one country or any particular stage of development.

The Aging World and Social Changes

The world is aging and so are the countries in the world, a result of decreasing birth rates and death rates, improved medical advances, and the out-migration of younger members of the less developed nations. Coupled with these demographic changes are the changes in the family, the traditional mechanism for the care of the elderly (Kosberg & Garcia, 1991; Kosberg, 1992). There are more divorces and remarriages; mixed marriages; and decisions not to marry and/or to remain childless. Greater mobility (both internal and external migration) also has resulted in the increased possibility that the family may not be available to undertake its traditional caregiving responsibility for the older members of the family.

So, too, there has been significant economic changes that have adversely affected countries and families. The family unit can be under significant economic stress (perhaps with unemployment or underemployment) that requires all able-bodied adults to be employed outside the home. A related and most significant social factor in the world is the emancipation of women from the home as they pursue education and careers. Thus, the female member of the family, the traditional caregiver of the elderly, is less available to provide such care.

In addition, populations have become more mobile than ever before. Large scale urbanization has moved the generally younger members of traditionally rural countries to urban areas to escape poverty and seek employment opportunities. Groups have immigrated elsewhere in the world to seek educational and employment opportunities. Often, it is the older members of the nation who are left behind in such an exodus.

Modernization in the World

Modern health technologies, scientific procedures in economic production and distribution, urbanization, and the extension of literacy and mass education have severely challenged the traditional way of life and values of the less developed countries of the world. Cowgill and Holmes (1972) suggest that, as countries become more modernized, the importance of the elderly in society is reduced. According to this view, the less developed countries treat the elderly with more respect, have more roles for them, and accord them higher status. In more developed nations, they are treated with less respect, have fewer roles to play, and hold a lower status in society.

Recent changes in one country in the Far East, an example of modernization and its impact (Kosberg & Kwan, 1989), included increases in working women, divorce and separation, in remarriages and mixed marriages (by race and religion), in gender equality (in education and employment), in the desire for children to live apart from their aging parents, in the freedom for mate selection, and in decisions regarding the size of one's own family. The consequences of such changes affect the composition and responsibilities of contemporary families in society.

Despite widespread support for the Modernization Theory, it has more recently been modified (in the face of challenges). Palmore and Manton (1974) suggested that while the status of the elderly does decline in the early stages of modernization, after a period of modernization has occurred, there is a tendency for the status of the elderly to stabilize and then rise. This improvement is the result of actions such as the growth of new programs to replace the farm and the family in maintaining the status of the elderly (retirement benefits, more adult education and job retraining, policies against age discrimination in employment, etc.). Cowgill (1974), too, revised his earlier theory.

The impact of such changes on family caregiving to the elderly are many and affect the existence, quality and quantity, availability, suitability, and desirability of family caregiving. This is to suggest that the social, demographic, and cultural changes in countries adversely affect the continuation of the family as a panacea in the care of the elderly. Overstressed, unmotivated, and ill-prepared family members may prove to be ineffective caregivers. It is also believed that such caregivers might engage in elder abuse.

SOCIAL AND CULTURAL CHANGES RELATED TO ELDER ABUSE

While the number of articles on elder abuse has increased over the past few years, much more has been written about the pressures on traditional family care of the elderly. Although not referring to elder abuse, per se, the situations discussed in such articles can well be signs of the problem and indicative of the growing existence of elder abuse. For example, reports on Nepal (Goldstein & Beale, 1982; Goldstein et al., 1983) alluded to "a cautionary tale from South Asia" resulting from the social and economic forces affecting intergenerational relationships in extended families in this Third-World country. Another article (Cheung, 1988) entitled "Implications of the One-Child Family Policy in . . . the People's Republic of China" suggested possible adverse consequences in the future for the traditional family care responsibilities. An article on Japanese attitudes toward the elderly (Koyano, 1989) stated that there was a discrepancy between "tatamae"–culturally-defined normative "shall" attitudes and "honne"–actual feelings toward caregiving responsibility. The "American idealization of aging" led to a courtesy custom without substance in Japan.

In a book on *Family Care of the Elderly: Social and Cultural Changes* (Kosberg, 1992) that includes chapters written by authors from 16 countries in the world, reference was made to elder abuse in only a few chapters. However, all the authors alluded to conditions that could very well be related to elder abuse. The following is a summary of the dynamics affecting family care of the elderly (and the possibilities for elder abuse) found in the 16 countries represented in the book.

- In the three "young" countries (Ghana, Mexico, and Thailand) with less than 4% of the population elderly, poverty, migration, and adverse economic conditions are affecting the traditional family structure and responsibilities.
- In the three "youthful" countries (China, Costa Rica, and Egypt) with between 5% and 7% of the population elderly, there is decreasing family size, poverty and unemployment, and mobility resulting in large proportions of impoverished elderly in rural areas.
- In the three "adult" countries (Argentina, Hong Kong, and Israel) with between 8% and 10% of the population elderly, independence of the elderly is being challenged by economic problems and a clash between traditional and contemporary values.
- In the four "mature" countries (Australia, Greece, Japan, and the United States) with between 11% and 14% of the population elderly, family care of the elderly is less likely because of the increasing size of the elderly population, emigration, changes in the value for filial piety, and the emancipation of women from the home.
- In the three "aged" countries (Austria, Great Britain, and Sweden) with 15% and more of the population elderly, the independence of the elderly is challenged by economic conditions that are adversely affecting their old age pensions, excessive reliance of female caregivers is causing problems in family caregiving, and formal welfare assistance is being strained by the growth of the elderly in hard economic times.

TRADITIONAL CONTROL MECHANISMS FOR FAMILY CAREGIVING

Family caregiving of the elderly has been sustained over time by a variety of mechanisms, from informal norms and mores to more formalized laws and policies. The latter group of enforcement mechanisms mandate and require families to care for their elderly relatives. Such formal policies have seldom been seen in contemporary societies. In the U.S., legislation for family caregiving requirements has been determined to be unconstitutional in states that possessed such statutes (Garrett, 1980). Even in those countries that have legislated family responsibility, there has been great difficulty in enforcing the law (Gibson, 1984).

Informal mechanisms to sustain family caregiving of the elderly are probably more effective than are the formal mechanisms. The influence of religious teachings and sanctions by friends and relatives are considered to be more powerful. Yet, several of the chapters within the book on family caregiving in the world (Kosberg, 1992) noted the changes that are adversely affecting the informal system for family caregiving of the elderly. For example, in a Buddhist country (Thailand) that has embraced ancestor worship, divorce, geographic mobility, and smaller family size are challenging traditional social relationships. Although the Koran influences the daily life of Moslem Egyptians, the family is undergoing changes (resulting from poverty and emigration) that are affecting its ability to care for the elderly. The Confucius teaching in China is undergoing revisions. Despite the fact that the Judeo-Christian admonition to honor one's father and mother is still valued in places such as Israel, the United States, and Mexico, authors from these countries described a growing lack of desire and/or inability to implement such a commandment.

Even village life, which had been glamorized as a location in which reciprocity and mutual concern provided supportive environments for the elderly, has undergone considerable change. The migration of younger members of a society have generally taken them from rural to urban areas, thus, leaving behind increasingly elderly populations (with fewer younger members for their informal support systems); and in urban areas, the elderly have been adversely affected by victimization and by new urban social norms that have influenced their younger relatives (and lessened the desire to take on caregiving responsibilities). Finally, Ken Tout (1989), in his book *Aging in Developing Countries*, concluded his analysis of aging in many countries of the world by suggesting that even religion could not be relied upon to "stay the process of disintegration" (p. 15) of marriage and the family in many (if not all) countries he studied in the East, Africa, and South America.

ELDER ABUSE IN THE WORLD

With more and more being written about elder abuse in the world, the question arises whether the problem is a relatively new one that is being discovered for the first time, whether it has always existed and is now increasing and can no longer be ignored, or whether it has always existed but is now the subject of study and practice. Although the consensus is that the problem of elder abuse has always existed, the demographic, social, and economic factors probably have led to a significant increase in the problem. In addition, of course, there has been an increase in the awareness of the problem influenced by research from the United States, Canada, and Great Britain.

As an example of the increased attention to elder abuse worldwide, the *Journal of Elder Abuse & Neglect*, over the past three years, has had articles from Japan (Kaneko & Yamada, 1990), Norway and elsewhere in Western Europe (Hydle, 1989), Australia (Sadler & Kurrie, 1993), Finland (Kivela et al., 1992), and Israel (Neikrug & Ronen, 1993), along with those from the United States, Canada, and Great Britain. In 1992 the Council on Europe published the report "Violence against elderly people" (SGVAEP, 1992) which focused on elder abuse as a form of intra-family violence. Facts, figures, and vignettes on such family violence in 15 European countries were presented.

Generally speaking, the definitions of elder abuse in the work by foreign authors have conformed to definitions established in North America. They have included physical abuse, psychological abuse, financial theft or misappropriation, active and passive neglect, and denial of rights. While the majority of studies have limited elder abuse discussions to adversities occurring within the community and perpetrated by members of one's informal support system (family, friends, and neighbors), in some instances, elder abuse includes adversities occurring within institutional settings and abusers who are volunteers and/or paid formal caregivers.

Nevertheless, the problem remains somewhat of a hidden issue. As Kosberg (1986) has written, elder abuse is one of the most invisible social problems in a society. It most frequently occurs within the privacy of the home and is viewed to be a family affair, generally not reported by the elderly victim, not identified, or mis-identified; for example, resulting from the frail condition of the older person.

Additionally, there are cultural reasons why the problem remains invisible within a country and not reported (in government documents, mass media, and scientific journals). It may be a taboo subject in some countries; namely those that emphasize a religious respect for the elderly. Further, a problem is not a problem unless it is detected and labelled as such. If elder abuse is not addressed and identified as a problem within a country then it is, ipso facto, not a problem for that country (even though the victims may continue to suffer). Moreover, should the conditions within a country adversely affect all citizens alike (infants, children, adults, and elderly), then it is likely that the elderly will not be singled out for special concern and attention.

As has been mentioned, westernization and cultural changes are occurring in many countries around the world. Most countries are aging, and the number and proportion of the elderly are increasing. This demographic reality is taking place along with increases in mobility, emigration, economic recessions, and changing characteristics of the family. For all of these reasons, it can be assumed that there will be an increase in the problem of elder abuse in the world.

ORGANIZATION OF BOOK

This book of readings on elder abuse around the world has resulted from the growing interest and work of those in the helping professions and from academia in different nations. In addition to the increase in publications on elder abuse, there has been wider representation of countries in the world at international forums on the problem. A 1986 international workshop in Jerusalem attended by persons from six countries, a 1987 seminar for the five nordic countries in Oslo, and a paper session on elder abuse at the 1989 International Congress of Gerontology with presentations from the U.S., Hong Kong, Japan, Mexico, Norway, and Denmark are examples of increasing attention on the world stage.

To ensure some degree of commonality among the countries

(chapters) discussed in the book, each author was asked to address the following topics: (1) the definition of elder abuse in the country, (2) the extent of the problem, (3) causes of the problem (as related to values and practices), (4) societal attitudes regarding the existence of the problem, and (5) private and public efforts to prevent the problem, to detect the existence of the problem, and intervene once the problem has occurred, and (6) policies developed to combat the problem. To be sure, addressing these issues necessitates a relatively well-developed understanding of and response to elder abuse in a country. Accordingly, the authors were asked to address each of the areas to the best of their ability.

The countries included in this collection are Australia, Finland, Greece, Hong Kong, India, Ireland, Israel, Norway, Poland, and South Africa. It is obvious that the following chapters do not represent either a random sample of all the countries in the world, nor are they representative of countries by continent, level of development, predominant religion, or proportion of elderly population. Thus, the findings and conclusions to be made (in the last chapter of the book) are not to be generalized but to be suggestive. As such, this book is perceived to be an antecedent effort at exploring the commonalities and unique features (regarding elder abuse) within and between the countries. Hopefully, too, this book will be useful for those from other countries in the world as they wrestle with the complexities of elder abuse.

REFERENCES

Australian Journal on Ageing. (1993). Special issue on elder abuse, *12*(4).

Beck, C.M. & Phillips, L.R. (1983). Abuse of the elderly. *Journal of Gerontological Nursing, 9*(2), 97-101.

Burston, G.G. (1975). Granny bashing. *British Medical Journal, 6*, 592.

Champlin, L. (1982). The battered elderly. *Geriatrics, 37*(7), 115-117.

Chan, P.H.T. (1985). *Report of elder abuse at home in Hong Kong.* Hong Kong Council of Social Services and Hong Kong Polytechnic.

Cheung, F.C.H. (1988). Implications of the one-child family policy on the development of the welfare state in the People's Republic of China. *Journal of Sociology and Social Welfare, XV*(1), 5-25.

Chow, N.W.S. (1983). The Chinese family and support of the elderly in Hong Kong. *The Gerontologist, 23*(6), 584-588.

Cowgill, D.O. & Holmes, L.D. (1972). (Eds.) *Aging and modernization*, New York: Meredith Corporation.

Cowgill, D.O. (1975). Aging and modernization: A revision of the theory. In J. Gubruim (Ed.), *Later life*, Springfield, IL: Charles C Thomas, 123-145.

Garrett, W.W. (1980). Filial responsibility laws. *Journal of Family Law, 18*, 793-818.

Gibson, M.J. (1984). Family support patterns, policies, and programs. *Innovative aging programs abroad: Implications for the United States* (edited by C. Nusberg), Westport, Conn: Greenwood Press, 159-195.

Goldstein, M.C. & Beall, C.M. (1982). Indirect modernization and the status of the elderly in a rural Third World setting. *Journal of Gerontology, 37*, 743-748.

Goldstein, M.C., Schuler, S. & Ross J.L. (1983). Social and economic forces affecting intergenerational relations in extended families in a Third World country: A cautionary tale from South Asia. *Journal of Gerontology, 38*(6), 716-724.

Hydle, I. (1989). Violence against the elderly in Western Europe–Treatment and preventive measures in the health and social service fields. *Journal of Elder Abuse & Neglect, 1*(3),75-87.

Johns, S., Hydle, I., & Aschjem, O. (1991). The act of abuse: A two-headed monster of injury and offense. *Journal of Elder Abuse & Neglect, 3*(1), 53-64.

Johns, S., Hydle, I., & Aschjem, O. (1989). The act of abuse: A two-headed monster of injury and offense. Paper presented at the Adult Protective Services Conference, San Antonio, Texas.

Kaneko, Y. & Yamada, Y. (1990). Wives and mothers-in-law: Potential for family conflict in post-war Japan. *Journal of Elder Abuse & Neglect, 2*(1&2), 87-99.

Kaneko, Y. (1987). *Rohjin-Gyakutai (Elder Abuse)*. Tokyo: Seiwa Press.

Kivelä, S.-L., Kongäs-Saviaro, P., Kesti, E., Pahkala, K., and Iäjs, M.-L. (1992). Abuse in old age-Epidemiological data from Finland. *Journal of Elder Abuse & Neglect, 4*(3), 1-18.

Kosberg, J.I. & Kwan, A.Y.H. (1989). *Elder abuse in Hong Kong and the United States: A comparative analysis with international implications.* Paper presented at a Symposium on Cross-Cultural Perspectives on Elder Abuse. International Congress of Gerontology. Acapulco, Mexico.

Kosberg, J.I. (1988). Preventing elder abuse: Identification of high risk factors prior to placement decisions. *The Gerontologist, 28*(1), 43-50.

Kosberg, J.I., (Ed) (1992). *Family care of the elderly: Social and cultural Changes*, Newbury Park, CA: Sage Publications.

Kosberg, J.I., (Ed) (1983). *Abuse and maltreatment of the elderly: Causes and interventions*, Boston: John Wright-PSG, Inc.

Kosberg, J.I. (1986). Victimization of the elderly. *Domestic Violence and Public Health*. Hearings before the Subcommittee on Children, Families, Drugs and Alcoholism of the Committee on Labor and Human Resources. U.S. Senate, October 30, 1985, Washington, DC, USGPO, 93-94.

Kosberg, J.I. & Garcia, J.L. (1991). Social changes affecting family care of the elderly. *Bold*, journal of the United Nations International Institute on Aging, *1*(2), 2-5.

Koyano, W. (1989). Japanese attitudes toward the elderly: A review of research findings. *Journal of Cross-Cultural Gerontology, 4*, 335-345.

Neikrug, S.M. & Ronen, M. (1993). Elder abuse in Israel. *Journal of Elder Abuse & Neglect, 5*(3), 1-19.

Palmore, E. (1975). The status and integration of the aged in Japanese society. *Journal of Gerontology, 30*, 199-208.

Palmore, E. & Manton, K. (1974) Modernization and status of the aged: International correlations. *Journal of Gerontology, 29*, 205-210.

Phillips, L.R. (1986). Theoretical explanations of elder abuse: Competing hypotheses and unresolved issues. In K.A. Pillemer and R.S. Wolf (eds.) *Elder Abuse: Conflict in the family.* Dover, MA: Auburn House Publishing Company.

Pillemer K.A. & Finkelhor, D. (1988). The prevalence of elder abuse: A random sample survey, *The Gerontologist, 28*(1), 51-57.

Quinn, M.J. & Tomita, S.K. (1986). *Elder abuse and neglect: Causes, diagnosis, and intervention strategies.* New York: Springer Publishing Company.

Ross, M. Ross, P.A. & Ross-Carson. (1985). Elder abuse in North America. *The Canadian Nurse,* 37-39.

Sadler, P.M. & Kurrie, S.E. (1993). Australian service providers' responses to elder abuse. *Journal of Elder Abuse & Neglect, 5*(1), 57-75.

Stang, G. & Evensen, A.R. (1985). Eldrfemishankling frem i lyset (Abuse of the elderly exposed). *Tidsskr Nor Laegeforen nr.* 34-35-36, 105: 2475-2478.

(SGVAEP) Study Group on Violence Against Elderly People, Council of Europe (1992). *Violence against elderly people.* Strasborg: Council of Europe Press.

Tornstam, L. (1987). Abuse of elderly in Denmark and Sweden: Results from a population study. Unpublished paper from the University of Copenhagen, Institute of Social Medicine, Copenhagen, Denmark.

Tout, K. (1989). *Aging in developing countries.* Oxford: Oxford University Press.

U.S. Congress, House Select Committee on Aging (1980). *Elder abuse: The hidden problem.* Washington, DC: United States Government Printing Office.

Chapter 2

'Elder Abuse' as an Innovation to Australia: A Critical Overview

Peter F. Dunn, MSocSci

Social and economic pressures over the last decade have influenced Australian governments to focus on policies that address the needs of the older population. Although public assistance to older Australians dates back nearly a century, the 1980s saw unprecedented attention to and reform of public policies for the aged (Kendig, 1990; Rowland, 1991). This focus on the 'greying' of the nation encouraged the development of research initiatives into the needs of older persons. The recognition of 'elder abuse' as a social construct and innovation to Australia coincided with this general focus on the aged; in particular, the vulnerable aged population.

THE CHANGING FACE OF AUSTRALIA

The face of the Australian population is rapidly showing signs of ageing. This transformation arises from increases in life expectancy

Peter F. Dunn is Lecturer, School of Humanities and Social Sciences, Charles Sturt University, Wagga Wagga, New South Wales, Australia.

[Haworth co-indexing entry note]: "'Elder Abuse' as an Innovation to Australia: A Critical Overview." Dunn, Peter F. Co-published simultaneously in the *Journal of Elder Abuse & Neglect* (The Haworth Press, Inc.) Vol. 6, No. 3/4, 1995, pp. 13-30; and: *Elder Abuse: International and Cross-Cultural Perspectives* (ed: Jordan I. Kosberg and Juanita L. Garcia) The Haworth Press, Inc., 1995, pp. 13-30. Multiple copies of this article/chapter may be purchased from The Haworth Document Delivery Center [1-800-3-HAWORTH; 9:00 a.m. - 5:00 p.m. (EST)].

13

and a reduction in both the birthrates and arrival of young migrants. Approximately 15 percent of its 17.5 million population were aged 60 years and over at the turn of this decade. Over the next 25 years the total population will grow by about 29 percent, those aged 65 and over will rise by 48 percent, those aged 75 years and over by 118 percent, and the population aged 85 and over by about 145 per cent (Graycar & Jamrozik, 1990). Australians currently have a life expectancy of 70 years for males and 77 years for females with a projected life expectancy at age 65 of 14 years for males in 2031 and 20 years for females (Rowland, 1991). The most vulnerable aged population, the 'old-old,' those over 75 years, comprise the most rapidly increasing group. The indigenous Aboriginal and Torres Strait Islander population comprise approximately 1.4 percent of the nation's population, with the proportion of aged over 50 years numbering around 20,000 or 9 percent (Commonwealth Department of Health Housing and Community Services, 1991). Available data reveal the Aboriginal life expectancy is significantly lower, as much as 20 years, below the non-Aboriginal population (Department of Immigration, Local Government and Ethnic Affairs, 1988). Substantial numbers of aged migrants from non-English speaking countries contribute to the changing face of the Australian population. The ethnic aged represent about 16 percent of the population aged 60 years and over, projected to increase to 22 percent by the year 2001. Most older Australians reside in metropolitan areas, although approximately one-third of the elderly live outside the major urban centers in largely rural and remote areas.

Living at Home

Australian older people generally want to age in their single family home with a preference for a 'modified-extended family' relationship (Rowland, 1991). The older relatives maintain contact with and accept support from family members who live apart from them, preserving independence without withdrawal from family involvement. One of the most common living arrangements, for a third of women and three-quarters of men, is with a spouse. Significant numbers of the population are reaching old age married and, hence, represent a prolongation of married life. Less common living arrangements are living alone or as a couple with others in the household. In comparison to the U.S. and the U.K., less elderly in Australia (13 percent of men and 31 percent of women aged 65 years and over) are likely to live alone (Rowland, 1991). For those living with others, the accommodation is usually shared with adult children or, to a lesser extent, siblings. The decision to live with younger relatives is often made to avoid the high costs of independent accommodation or due to frailty (Rowland, 1991; Commonwealth Department of Health, Housing and Community Services, 1991).

Some 40 percent of carers of the dependent elderly are wives, 33 percent are husbands, 16 percent are daughters, 5 percent are sons, and 7 percent are other relatives or friends (Commonwealth Department of Health, Housing, and Community Services, 1991). The primary carers for men are wives (91%), while women have their husbands as carers in 60 percent of households. Daughters play a significant role as carers of the 'old-old,' representing 10 percent of the co-resident carers for people 70 years and older which increases to 30 percent for co-resident carers of handicapped people aged 75 years and older (Australian Institute of Health, 1990). The 'old-old' age group corresponds with widowhood and the onset of infirmity. Without a spouse to assume the role of carer, aged widows increasingly feel pressure to move in with adult offspring or relocate to more convenient premises (Rowland, 1991).

RECOGNITION OF ELDER ABUSE AS AN INNOVATION

Older people as victims of crime, abuse, and exploitation has largely been an innovation for Australia over the last decade. Following developments in other countries, principally the U.S. and the U.K., Australia sought to identify new social issues relating to its maturing population. This led to a focus on the plight of the vulnerable aged by policy-makers, academics, and service providers. Among the related social innovations were fear of crime and victimization of the elderly (Biles, 1983) and the abuse of residents of residential care institutions (Ronalds, 1989). During the 1980s the concept of 'aged victims' was limited to incidents of crime, exploitation, or abuse by persons other than family or informal caregivers, and cases of abuse, intimidation, and violation of rights within residential care facilities. The abuse and neglect of older persons by family members had gone unrecognized or, more importantly, unlabelled. Coinciding with public acknowledgement of these two issues were developments in child abuse and domestic violence including a weakening resistance by the public and government to explore family violence.

Efforts to raise the issue of aged victimization in the home during the 1970s and 1980s were both few and unsuccessful. A Federal Government recommendation on the establishment of coordinated protective services (Social Welfare Commission, 1975) and criticisms by a state Council on the Ageing of inaction on aged mistreatment (Duncan, 1981) were met with further inaction. It was not until 1986 that an aged abuse conference in the state of Victoria aroused the interest of the Office of the Public Advocate (OPA), although it failed to attract the attention of policy makers. The OPA, a state government agency, went on to develop, implement, and report on a study of the abuse of older people in the community (Barron et al., 1990).

Placing Elder Abuse on the Agenda

Dunn (1993) argued that elder abuse in Australia attained the public agenda in the early 1990s due to the merging of at least five factors: the release of the OPA community study, 'No Innocent Bystanders'; the activities of some state agencies responsible for the interests of older persons (such as the establishment of committees of inquiry into aged abuse); the establishment, Australia-wide, of multidisciplinary aged care assessment teams and the resultant information exchange; the heightened coverage of related news items by the media; and the publication of articles on elder abuse in *The Medical Journal of Australia* and the resultant public attention and press coverage. This last factor is arguably the most critical in the development of elder abuse as an issue in Australia. Kurrle et al., (1992, p.674) report that the abuse of the elderly "was first brought to the attention of the Australian medical profession in August 1991 with a report of 15 cases of physical abuse and neglect." Reluctance by the Australian medical profession to acknowledge the abuse of older persons has been cited by several authors (Duncan, 1981, Barron et al., 1990, Dunn & Hanrahan,

1990, Kurrle et al.,1992) and perhaps arises from claims of ageism that allegedly plague the Australian medical profession (Rowland, 1991).

Defining the Problem

The rise of elder abuse in Australia has been strongly influenced by developments in the United States. Both the goals of research on elder abuse in Australia and the definition or construction of the problem show a 'heavy influence and dependence on research from the United States' (Dunn, 1993, p. 10). Several authors have adopted similar categories of elder abuse as those generally utilized by researchers and policymakers in the U.S., e.g., physical and psychological abuse, financial/economic exploitation, and neglect (Barron et al., 1990; Dunn & Hanrahan, 1990; Office of the Commissioner for the Ageing, 1993; Kurrle et al., 1991; McCallum et al., 1990). Definitions of elder abuse vary in the Australian literature from a description of each category (Barron et al., 1990; Kurrle et al., 1991) to a broad statement within which all categories are comprised. The latter, for example, includes defining elder abuse as "any pattern of behavior by a person that results in physical or psychological harm to an older person" (McCallum et al., 1990, p. 11). It has been argued that the dependence on foreign definitions and research has led to a distortion in the construction of the problem in Australia (Dunn, 1993; McDermott, 1993). This distortion arises from adopting a label that was constructed within an alien culture and defined for the purposes of a foreign government (Dunn, 1993).

More recent attention to elder abuse has, however, created a number of variations to overseas definitions. Some research overlooks the need to define the context or setting of abuse, such as whether abuses, so classified, include those in private dwellings, institutions, or the community at-large. Kurrle et al. (1991), for example, fail to offer an explanation of the setting within which the term 'elder abuse' applies, yet make comparisons with research in the U.S. where it generally refers to domestic settings. 'Self neglect' or 'self abuse,' while comprising a type of neglect in many of the reports in the U.S., has tended to be excluded from Australian categories (NSW Taskforce on Abuse of Older People, 1992;

Kurrle et al., 1992; Office of the Commissioner for the Ageing, 1992). In addition, the Australian literature displays sensitivity in generally avoiding the setting of strict age criterion which acknowledged that chronological age does not in itself imply others may not have similar needs (e.g., Aboriginal person's life expectancy is about 20 years lower than in the general community and some Alzheimer's sufferers are in their 50s).

EXTENT OF THE PROBLEM

The placement of an issue on the social agenda often requires, as a political imperative, a determination of the size and nature of the problem. However, owing to its recent recognition, the diversity in definitions and research complexities, very few Australian studies have been undertaken. Three published studies of service providers (Barron et al., 1990; McCallum et al., 1990; Kurrle & Sadler, 1993) and two agency case reviews (Kurrle et al., 1991; 1992) have provided testimony of the existence of abuse of older persons in the Australian community and contribute to a description of the extent of the problem. Unfortunately, however, due to inadequate methodology related to sampling and variations in the context of abuse, reliable comparisons cannot be made.

McCallum et al. (1990) sought to determine the 'range' of the problem of abuse as perceived by service providers in a region of Adelaide in South Australia. Apart from the service providers' sensitivity to the issue, they reported predominantly physical and economic abuses. In contrast, Barron et al. (1990), in their Melbourne study, reported physical abuse as the least common and economic abuse the most often recalled type. The abused persons were identified as predominantly female, in their 70s and 80s, with approximately a third coming from a non-English speaking background and the majority having a low proficiency in English. The authors concluded that there is evidence that "far more abuse is suspected or is actively recognized than is ever reported" (Barron et al., 1990, p. 27). Inconsistencies between the findings of these studies are largely a by-product of the methodology and the orientation of the researchers.

Kurrle and Sadler (1993) surveyed service providers in two local government areas of Sydney, New South Wales and reported that the majority of those who responded were unaware of cases of elder abuse. Of those who could recall incidents, psychological abuse was the most frequently observed. In a related study, Kurrle et al. (1992) reviewed the medical records of a geriatric and rehabilitation service for a 12 month period in an attempt to establish a rate of occurrence. They found a rate of 4.6 percent in the study population with psychological and physical abuse being the most common. The victims were described as generally frail and dependent with a significant proportion of them diagnosed with physical disabilities (64.8%) and dementia (46.3%). Despite claims otherwise, the findings cannot be generalized due to a sampling bias.

In determining those older persons more at-risk of abuse, the Australian research on elder abuse has many shortcomings. Fortunately, however, several studies on the vulnerabilities of older Australians may assist in identifying the extent of the problem, given that the "distribution of vulnerabilities varies sharply among social groups in later life according to sex, class, ethnicity, and race" (Kendig, 1990, p. 7). Older women have been clearly identified in the overseas literature, and this is supported in the limited Australian research, as those older persons more likely to be victims of abuse, neglect, and exploitation. However, this is hardly surprising given the observation that "when we discuss the elderly we are often talking about what is essentially a women's issue" (Barron et al., 1990, p. 9).

A review of the Australian literature on ageing identifies further subgroups of elderly persons who may be more vulnerable, or 'at-risk,' to abusive, exploitative, or neglectful situations, including self-neglect: widows, aged migrants, disabled/frail persons, the Aboriginal and Torres Strait Islander aged population, isolates, medication users, rural and remote dwellers, and the poor. The concept of 'vulnerability' is a more appropriate starting point for the examination and social construction of abuse of older persons in Australia than the indiscriminate adoption of 'elder abuse' as developed in the United States. The lesson to learn from the United States is that there are likely to be subgroups in society who are at higher risk of exposure to abuse, neglect, and exploitation at the hands of family members and friends.

IN SEARCH OF A REASON

Despite a decade of research in the United States on elder abuse and related issues, Wolf and Pillemer (1989) conclude that "a theoretical framework for understanding elder abuse cannot be derived from previous research on elder abuse" (p. 22). For similar reasons, the scant research in Australia does not allow the development of theories to explain the reasons for the mistreatment of older persons. The research does provide evidence that older persons are the victims of abuse, exploitation, and neglect. However, as commented earlier, few comparisons can be made with the results due to differences in definitions, methodology, and assumptions about the nature of abuse.

The validity of the majority of the research is of dubious value as the methodology relies upon service provider recall and the interpretation of alleged abuse incidents. Researchers have failed, in most cases, to confirm reported cases of abuse accepting them to be authenticated by reference to a definition and list of categories. The study by Kurrle et al. (1991) involved a retrospective review of patients of the geriatric and rehabilitation unit attached to a district hospital. The researchers labeled cases involving soft tissue damage or fractures as 'elder abuse' because they met the requirements of their predetermined definition and concluded that "there is no doubt that abuse had occurred in the cases we detected" (p. 152). However, experiences in the U.S. indicate that some normal changes in the bodies of older persons or injuries caused by 'falls and balance' problems are sometimes mistaken for signs of abuse or neglect (Washington, 1992). Given that over one third of all disabled persons in institutional care were injured at home and that injuries are most common among persons aged over 70 years, it would be advisable that researchers acknowledge a "continuum rather than a sharp distinction between intentional and unintentional injuries" (Australian Institute of Health, 1990, p. 223).

Cautionary comments aside, victimization of older persons does occur, and a few Australian authors have speculated on its causes. Barron et al. (1990) believe that a quest to identify a single predominant cause would be 'fruitless.' They suggest that the psychopathology of the abuser or the abused may be a precipitating factor. However, the more significant causes are likely to arise from three areas: firstly, community attitudes towards the ageing population; secondly, the lack of community education and awareness about aged abuse; and, finally, the dearth of education, training, and support available to carers, relatives, and service providers.

Barron et al. (1990) are critical that few commentators have considered abuse in the context of broader theories of violence that rely on individual pathology as an explanation. They argue that abuse of older people arises from "the inequality in power relationships between those seen to be competitive, wealth producing, and dominant on the one hand, and those seen to be passive, consuming, and dependent on the other" (Barron et al., 1990, p. 59). Despite arguments that ageism and its related negative stereotypes are no longer a serious obstacle to the provision of public support to the aged in Australia (Rowland, 1991), ageism, along with sexism, are considered societal values that pervade Australian institutions such as the legal, welfare, education, and health systems. Australia should not view the search for a single causal factor as the priority but should give a critical examination of broader social causes for the victimization of vulnerable persons.

Etiology and the Burden of Care

Attention to the etiology of elder abuse in Australia is founded on naivety and presumption. How is it that a cause can be determined for a social problem which has not yet been adequately defined or established? Carer stress as a cause of abuse or mistreatment has been reported primarily as speculation rather than a research finding (Rowland, 1991; Duncan, 1981; Australian Institute of Health, 1990). Rowland (1991) draws on an analysis of Australia's ageing population, the 'gerontological transition,' to argue that increasing numbers of families will bear the responsibility to care for their frail aged relatives and will create a 'dependency squeeze.' This increased responsibility on family will be met with a decrease in the availability of relatives and informal support. Thus, the abuse of the elderly "by their carers is likely to become more prevalent towards the end of the transition, because of widespread stresses entailed in supporting the frail at home" (Rowland, 1991, p. 199). The ramifications–emotionally, physically, and financially–to the carer of a dependent older relative have been acknowledged by Australian researchers and are reflected in various policies and programs (Braithwaite, 1986; Brodaty & Gresham, 1989; Commonwealth Department of Health Housing and Community Services, 1991; Kendig, 1991; Rossiter et al., 1984).

Increased dependency can result in major changes in living arrangements that can expose the older person to mistreatment. While many older Australians enjoy 'intimacy at a distance,' it is usually the reserve of the healthy and mobile. The frail aged often having to "accept a degree of contact and involvement with relatives that is well above or well below the average" (Rowland, 1991, p. 114). Due to insufficient alternatives, the older person, in particular a widow, may have to reside with a daughter, son, or other family member or a family member moves in with the older relative. Should the provision of care by family not be the result of careful deliberation, then they may find themselves in situations that may lead to abuse (Barron et al., 1990). Other findings suggest that while carer stress was present, it was only one of several risk factors; dependency and the psychopathology of the abuser were more significant causes (Kurrle et al., 1991; 1992). The search for a reason for elder abuse will not, however, be advanced by presumption. Until there is a degree of unanimity about the construction of the problem, there is a danger of the legitimation of some reported causes of abuse and neglect. This could conceivably result in poor decision-making in the development of policies, programs, and services in response to the problem.

CONSIDERING THE RESPONSE OPTIONS

Australia has not evolved a system for the protection of vulnerable older persons. More specifically, there are no integrated services that can be described as 'adult protective services' in the context in which the term is used currently in the U.S. Various legal and social service remedies can, however, be utilized, in some cases to protect the rights or interests of the vulnerable individual. As will be discussed later, some sectors of the Australian community display a reluctance to institute new mechanisms in response to increased awareness of abuse. The issue is so poorly defined and the research so limited and contradictory, it is not surprising that responses have been mindful but clearly prudent. The trend has been to consider policy and program response options and to reinforce the utilization of existing services and programs in contrast to the development of new legislation. An existing service acknowledged as having a legitimate role in responding to alleged cases of elder abuse is adult guardianship.

Guardianship and Advocacy

Significant changes in adult guardianship have essentially been restricted to the past 20 years and are reported to have arisen out of developments on human rights by the United Nations and research emanating from the U.S. (Logan, 1991). While older persons were not excluded, persons with an intellectual disability were the primary focus of guardianship reform. However, more recently, such reform has been recognized as having a significant role in the protection of older persons from abuse and neglect (Barron et al., 1990, Dunn, 1990; Kurrle et al., 1992; NSW Taskforce on Abuse of Older People, 1992). Each of the six states and two territories comprising the Commonwealth of Australia are either reviewing their provisions for adult guardianship or have already implemented new legislation. A further development is the introduction in 1992 of annual national conferences on guardianship and financial management.

The state of Victoria has been the most active in the pursuit of the protection of older persons from abuse and neglect. The 'Victorian model,' which has received both national and international recognition (Logan, 1991), comprises the Guardianship and Administration Board and the Office of the Public Advocate (OPA). The OPA has as its mission "to promote the rights and dignity of people with disabilities, to strengthen their position in society, and to reduce their exploitation, abuse and neglect" (OPA, 1991, p. v). Champion (1993) suggests that under the 'Victorian model,' "a whole range of services exist that can deal with various situations of maltreatment and neglect of older people. It is not necessary to set up a new protective system for older adults" (p. 10).

State and Federal Initiatives

As in the U.S., the Australian states have been more pro-active in the development of elder abuse as an issue than at the Federal level.

In three states, New South Wales (NSW), Victoria, and South Australia, the government office responsible for the interests of older persons has been central to raising public and political awareness. During 1992, the NSW Office on Ageing established the Task Force on the Abuse of Older People which distributed a public discussion paper and held statewide consultations before presenting recommendations to the government. In Victoria, the Older Person's Planning Unit formed a working party that submitted recommendations to the Victorian Government, and in South Australia, the Office of Commissioner for the Ageing funded a demonstration project on Elder Protection. In some of the other states and territories, the non-government sector has played a pivotal role in promoting the issue. The Council on the Ageing (COTA) in Western Australia, the Australian Capital Territory and the Northern Territory, and the Queensland Council of Carers, took initiatives with the support of government agencies to organise demonstration projects, conferences and to establish task forces.

The Federal Government has focused primarily on aged care reform, targeting vulnerable groups such as the frail aged, ethnic aged, Aboriginal older persons, and the aged population residing in rural and remote areas of Australia. Given the prominent role of the Federal Government in aged care reform, it is not surprising that state governments have actively sought to include elder abuse within their portfolio. The Federal Government, through its Department of Health, Housing and Community Services, has chosen to absorb the issue of aged mistreatment within its existing policy statements on 'residents rights' and 'user rights' (Queensland Taskforce on the Prevention of Intimidation and Abuse of the Elderly, 1993). In early 1993, however, the Federal Government announced its intention to establish a 'working party' to consider the protection of frail older persons. The announcement, which came within three weeks of a national election, signified an admission by the Federal Government that the abuse of older persons had been listed on the agenda.

Responding to an Enigma

Given the limited Australian research, associated methodology problems, and a growing debate over what constitutes elder abuse, there is much that is still unknown about the issue in this society. Proponents of the issue have sought public support for an enigma. The public and the state are being pressed to consider response options for a social problem that has been inadequately debated and constructed. Australia has paid too little attention to the need for an examination of the ethical, legal, and economic implications of elder abuse and related response options. For these reasons, it is perhaps understandable that action to date can best be described as prudent rather than hasty.

State recommendations have identified several priority issues. There is general consensus on the need to develop policies, protocols, and guidelines for workers in agencies involved with older persons. The demonstration projects in Western Australia and South Australia both aim to address this issue. The NSW Taskforce on Abuse of Older People included examples of agency protocols in response to allegations of elder abuse in their widely distributed public discussion paper (NSW Taskforce on Abuse of Older People, 1992). A significant national program, the Home and Community Care Program (HACC), is likely to be closely involved in the development of policy for the prevention, detection, and intervention of the abuse of older persons (Dunn & Hanrahan, 1990). The HACC Program, introduced in 1985, involves the broadening of community care and aged care assessment. It was designed to "provide consumers with a range of services which offer more opportunities to live independently for as long as possible and avoid inappropriate or premature admission to long-term residential care" (Minichiello et al., 1992, p. 146). The home care services provided under the program and the fact that HACC targets the frail aged, disabled, and their carers place workers in a unique position to detect, prevent, and intervene in cases of elder abuse (Queensland Taskforce on the Prevention of Intimidation and Abuse of the Elderly, 1993).

When considering response options, Australia has generally focused on five alternatives. Option A (Establish Investigative Body) is characterized by higher costs, a higher level of intervention, greater dilution of service agency responsibility, significant legislative reform, and less necessity for community coordination with the other options varying accordingly (Option D: Interagency Response Team; Option E: Maintain Status Quo with increased

Training and Awareness). Variations of Option C (Key Organizations Develop Internal Policies with Interagency Coordination) comprise the current response mechanism most often proposed; however, the issue of case management responsibility is found to be difficult to resolve. In the event that all health, welfare, and protective services institute policies and procedures, they will still require an agency to co-ordinate and generally assume responsibility. As a multidisciplinary team within the HACC Program, the Aged Care Assessment Teams (ACAT) have been suggested as a preferred existing service (Option B–Existing Agency Adopt Investigative Role) to receive referrals from the community (NSW Taskforce on Abuse of Older People 1992; Kurrle et al., 1992). Distributed nationally, the ACATs may play a detection and intervention role, necessitating the training of professionals including geriatricians, social workers, and occupational therapists.

Legislation that provides for mandatory reporting has not been debated and yet is considered favorably by some sectors of the community (NSW Taskforce on Abuse of Older People, 1993). Only a few commentators have considered the issue of mandatory reporting and each has opposed its introduction, especially at such an early stage of the issue's development (Dunn & Hanrahan, 1990; Kurrle et al., 1992; NSW Taskforce on Abuse of Older People, 1992). There appears to be popular opposition to the introduction of new legislation that exclusively deals with elder abuse, especially among state government offices on ageing (Champion, 1993; McDermott, 1993; NSW Office on Ageing, 1992). Preference is given to an examination of relevant existing legislation and, if deemed to be inappropriate, amendments to that legislation, e.g., family violence, guardianship, and criminal law. A further explanation for the apparently cautious approach by both government and non-government organizations responsible for aged advocacy is the perceived conflict of interests. As advocates, they promote the dismantling of ageism and challenge stereotypes of the elderly as vulnerable and incompetent. However, responding to the issue of elder abuse requires that they expose a subgroup of the aged population who are dependent, vulnerable, and in many cases incompetent. This conflict of interests may contribute to a cautious response.

THE FUTURE OF 'ELDER ABUSE' IN AUSTRALIA

Australian society has acknowledged that some of its aged population suffer abuse, neglect, and exploitation. This observation is
not contentious. What is contentious is the way Australia will define
and construct the problem and the types of responses initiated to
prevent, detect, and intervene and, finally, the order in which these
two take place. Such conflict should involve debate over ethical,
legal, and economic matters surrounding social intervention and the
protection of older persons. It will also contribute to a continued
interest in elder abuse as a social problem in the future. Other
factors include a general interest in the problems associated with an
ageing population, the involvement of the State and Federal Gov-
emments, increased allegations of aged victimization, and a bur-
geoning interest by professionals.

As the implications of an ageing population become more prominent, elder abuse, as an age related issue, may receive on-going
attention. In his analysis of the gerontological transition with
respect to Australia, Rowland (1991) assumes a close relationship
between the growth of the elderly population, variations in the
resources and needs of the aged, and a shift in the status of the
elderly in society. He argues that these interrelationships "lead to a
predictable sequence in the emergence of issues concerning the
aged, including the nature and extent of aged dependency, the ade-
quacy of family support, and the prevalence of ageism" (Rowland,
1991, p. 189). It is highly likely that the protection of older persons
will form one of those issues, given the current focus on elder
abuse, adult guardianship, service provision for the frail aged and
disabled, and recognition of the 'burden of care.' An ageing population could well signal increases in the proportion of vulnerable aged
subgroups, such as dependent widows, ethnic aged, indigenous
older people, and the chronic disabled; subgroups that may be more
likely at-risk to situations resulting in their victimization.

The Australian medical, health, and social welfare profession,
criminologists, and academics have already staked a claim on 'elder
abuse.' The role of professionals in placing elder abuse on the
agenda has been acknowledged in both the U.S. (Callahan, 1981;
Wolf & Pillemer, 1989) and Canada (Leroux & Petrunik, 1990). As

a professional concern, it is likely that pressure will be maintained on governments to act and recognize the problem. Calls for action may be supported by the growth in reporting of allegations of abuse and neglect that follow increased awareness and sensitivity by those who work with vulnerable older persons. One may feed the other, combining to lobby governments to act out of a sense of urgency, perhaps forcing the governments' hand before adequate debate has taken place, a process leading to a moral tragedy. Conversely, abuse of older persons may remain peripheral to the main agenda items of government for several years as economic restraint and rational policymaking hinder governments from funding new social programs. It may well remain a research interest area restricted to 'academics, policy analysts, and human service professionals' for some time before significant developments occur (Dunn, 1993).

In conclusion, it is apparent that 'elder abuse' as a social construct was an innovation to Australia originating in the U.S. Differences in health care provision, long term care programs, the legal system, not to mention cultural values, combine to make it imperative that the issue be critically assessed and researched in context. The real issue for Australia is not to adopt a new social problem, not to establish the 'Let's Prove the Same Problem Exists Here' Syndrome, but to be enlightened by overseas developments (Dunn, 1993). This should lead to the identification of those individuals in the population most vulnerable to mistreatment and victimization and ensure that suitable preventative and protective measures are accessible and well founded.

REFERENCES

Australian Institute of Health. (1990). *Australia's health 1990: The second biennial report of the Australian Institute of Health*. Canberra: Australian Government Publishing Service.

Barron, B., Cran, A., Flitcroft, J., McDermott, J. & Montague, M. (1990). *No innocent bystanders: A study of abuse of older people in our community*. Office of the Public Advocate, Melbourne.

Biles, D. (1983). Crime and the elderly. *Australian Journal of the Ageing*, 2(4), 22-23.

Braithwaite, V. (1987). Coming to terms with burden in home care. *Australian Journal on Ageing*, 6(1), 20-23.

Brodaty, H. & Gresham, M. (1989). Effects of a training program to reduce stress in carers of patients with dementia. *British Medical Journal, 299*, 1375-1379.

Champion, M. (1993). Advocacy, guardianship and administration in Victoria in *Proceedings of the Crime and Older People Conference*, 23-25 February, Adelaide, Australian Institute of Criminology, Canberra.

Commonwealth Department of Health, Housing and Community Services. (1991). *Aged care reform strategy: Mid-term review 1990-91 report.* Canberra: Australian Government Publishing Service.

Department of Immigration, Local Government and Ethnic Affairs. (1988). *Australia's population trends and prospects 1988*, Australian Government Publishing Service, Canberra.

Duncan, S. (1981). Domestic violence and the aged. *Institute of Criminology Proceedings, 54*, University of Sydney, Sydney, 107-113.

Dunn, P. F. (1993). The 'getting' of elder abuse on the agenda in *Proceedings of the Crime and Older People Conference*, 23-25 February, Adelaide, Australian Institute of Criminology, Canberra.

Dunn, P. F. & Hanrahan, C.F. (1990). Maltreatment of older persons in the home in *Proceedings of The Hospitals and Health Services Association of NSW*, 69th Annual Conference, Sydney.

Graycar, A. & Jamrozik, A. (1989). *How Australians live: Social policy in theory and practice.* South Melbourne: The Macmillan Company.

Kendig, H. (1990). Ageing, policies and politics. In H. Kendig & McCallum, J. (Eds.), *Grey policy: Australian policies for an ageing society* (1-22). Sydney: Allen and Unwin.

Kurrle, S. E., Sadler, P. M. & Cameron, I. (1991). Elder abuse–An Australian case series. *The Medical Journal of Australia, 155*, 150-153.

Kurrle, S.E., Sadler, P.M. & Cameron, I. (1992). Patterns of elder abuse. *The Medical Journal of Australia, 157*, 673-675.

Kurrle, S. E. & Sadler, P. M. (1993). Australian service providers: Responses to elder abuse. *Journal of Elder Abuse & Neglect, 5*(1), 57-76.

Leroux, T. G. & Petrunik, M. (1990). The construction of elder abuse as a social problem: A Canadian perspective. *International Journal of Health Services, 20*(4), 651-663.

Logan, B.(1991). A description of adult guardianship and implications for social work. *Australian Social Work, 44*(3), 19-29.

McCallum, J., Matiasz, S., & Graycar, A. (1990). *Abuse of the elderly at home: The range of the problem*, Office of the Commissioner for the Ageing, Adelaide.

McDermott, J.(1993). Elder abuse: Eight scenarios in search of a construct. In *Proceedings of the Crime and Older People Conference*, 23-25. February, Adelaide, Australian Institute of Criminology, Canberra.

Minichiello, V., Alexander, L., & Jones, D. (Eds.). (1992). *Gerontology: A multi-disciplinary approach.* Melbourne: Prentice Hall.

New South Wales Taskforce on Abuse of Older People. (1992). *Abuse of older people in their homes.* Office on Ageing, Sydney.

New South Wales Taskforce on Abuse of Older People. (1993). *Abuse of older people in their homes: Final report.* Office on Ageing, Sydney.

Office of the Commissioner for the Ageing. (1993). *Elder protection project,* Office of the Commissioner for the Ageing, Adelaide.

Queensland Taskforce on the Prevention of Intimidation and Abuse of the Elderly. (1993). *Dignity and security: The right of older persons.* Proceedings of the conference on the abuse and neglect of older persons, 30-31 October, Brisbane.

Ronalds, C. (1989). *I'm still an individual.* Department of Community Services and Health, Canberra.

Rossiter, C., Kinnear, D. & Graycar, A. (1984). Family care of elderly people: 1983 survey results in *SWRC Reports and Proceedings* No. 38, Social Welfare Research Center, University of New South Wales, Sydney.

Rowland, D.T. (1991). *Ageing in Australia.* Melbourne: Longman Cheshire.

Social Welfare Commission. (1975). *Care of the aged,* Social Welfare Commission, Canberra.

Washington, S. (1992). *Recognizing abuse in the midst of aging,* Workshop held at the Ninth Annual Adult Protective Services Conference, Conference Program, 12 November, Texas Department of Protective and Regulatory Services and the American Public Welfare Association, San Antonio.

Wolf, R.S. & Pillemer, K.A. (1989). *Helping elderly victims: The reality of elder abuse.* New York: Columbia University Press.

Chapter 3

Elder Abuse in Finland

Sirkka-Liisa Kivelä, MD

THE FINNISH ELDERLY POPULATION

Demographic Characteristics

At the end of 1990, the total Finnish population numbered approximately 5 million, of whom 13.5 percent were aged 65 years or over. The population aged 75 years or over accounted for 5.7 percent of the total population, and the population aged 85 years or over accounted for 1.0 percent (Statistics Finland, 1992). As these figures show, the age structure in Finland is quite similar to that of other western industrialized countries. However, the aging of the Finnish population started later than many other industrialized countries, the size and relative proportion of the population aged 65-74 years increased in the 1960s, those of the population aged 75-84 years in the 1970s, while the actual "greying" happened in the 1980s with the rapid growth of the population aged 85 years or over.

In ethnic terms, the population living in Finland is very homogeneous; among the elderly population, the number of people belong-

Sirkka-Liisa Kivelä is Professor, University of Oulu, Department of Public Health Science and General Practice, Aapistie 3, 90220 Oulu, Finland.

[Haworth co-indexing entry note]: "Elder Abuse in Finland." Kivelä, Sirkka-Liisa. Co-published simultaneously in the *Journal of Elder Abuse & Neglect* (The Haworth Press, Inc.) Vol. 6, No. 3/4, 1995, pp. 31-44; and: *Elder Abuse: International and Cross-Cultural Perspectives* (ed: Jordan I. Kosberg, and Juanita L. Garcia) The Haworth Press, Inc., 1995, pp. 31-44. Multiple copies of this article/chapter may be purchased from The Haworth Document Delivery Center [1-800-3-HAWORTH; 9:00 a.m. - 5:00 p.m. (EST)].

ing to other than the Finnish race is lower than in other age groups. Although there are two official languages in the country, the culture and norms do not vary much in different areas of Finland. The vast majority (93%) of the total population are Finnish-speaking, while 6 percent belong to the Swedish-speaking minority (Statistics Finland, 1992). The Evangelical Lutheran Church is, in effect, the state church in Finland with some 90 percent of the total population belonging to it. Just over 1 percent belong to the Greek Orthodox Church of Finland and 1 percent to the Roman Catholic Church (Statistics Finland, 1992).

Industrialization in Finland has occurred rather late and rapidly with the result that in the 1960s and 1970s there has been a considerable degree of internal migration from north to south and from the countryside into the towns. One indication of the speed of the change is the decline in the proportion of the agrarian population from 46 percent of the labor force in 1950 to a mere 6.9 percent in 1979. Due to the effects of migration, it is common to find that elderly parents and their middle-aged children live far away from each other (Statistics Finland, 1992).

The difference between the life-expectancy of Finnish men (70.9 years) and Finnish women (78.9 years) is one of the highest in the western world (Statistics Finland, 1992). This is clearly reflected in the statistics on the marital status of persons aged 65 years or over, which indicate that men are usually married (about 70 percent) and less often widowed (about one sixth), while women are likely to be widowed (about one half) and less often married (about one-third). Divorced elderly men (2%) and women (2%) who have not remarried account for a very small proportion of the elderly. About one in ten elderly men and women have never been married (Kivelä, 1993b).

The proportion of elderly persons with no surviving children is astonishingly high. Every tenth elderly man and woman belongs to the group of never-married with no surviving children. Out of the elderly population who have been married at least once, nearly 10 percent have no surviving children. Thus, every fifth elderly person in Finland has no children. For many elderly persons, children and their families are an important source of social contacts. For 20 percent of the elderly, no such support is available (Kivelä, 1993b).

If defining the family as consisting of the elderly person, the spouse, children, grandchildren, siblings, and mother and father, then the share of aged men in Finland with no family is low; fewer than 1 percent of men have no family. The proportion of elderly women without a family is quite high; altogether 6 percent of women cannot expect any social or concrete support from their families (Kivelä, 1993b). Families and other relatives are in important source of concrete and affective support of many Finnish elders, regardless of whether they also receive care through public sources. On average, Finnish elderly persons are satisfied with the informal support they receive through unofficial sources (Kivelä, 1993b).

The proportion of the population aged 65 years or over in long-term institutional care is quite high (8 percent). About half of Finland's elderly men and every fourth elderly woman live together with their spouse in a household consisting of only two persons. About every sixth man and every third woman lives alone. About every sixth man and woman lives in a household consisting of their spouses and other persons, and every sixth woman lives together with other persons without their spouses (Kivelä, 1993b).

Social and Health Care Services

Traditionally, the Finnish society has taken on much of the responsibility for the individual's welfare. Social and health care services are mainly operated by the local administrative units (viz. municipalities and towns) which are self-governing units with the right to levy taxes. The costs of social and health care services for the users are low and equal in all parts of the country because they are subsidized by the local administrative units and the state. In addition to official channels, Finland has a number of voluntary organizations that are actively involved in providing social services; this work is subsidized by the state. Welfare services are also arranged under the auspices of the Evangelical Lutheran Church.

There is also a private health and social sector in Finland which is subsidized by the state. Until the latter half of the 1980s, the amount of private services was still quite limited; the official policy was to give priority to the development of the services owned by the municipalities and towns. More emphasis has been placed on privatization in the late 1980s and early 1990s. At the same time, the resources allocated to public social and health care have been reduced; the trend now is to de-emphasize public services.

During the past 10 to 20 years, efforts in Finland have concentrated on promoting noninstitutional care by supporting living at home through sheltered housing, home nursing services, and home help services. In spite of these efforts, the proportion of the elderly population in long-term institutional care is quite high. During the past ten years, the figure has been about 8 percent of the population aged 65 years or over. Although the amount of sheltered houses, home nursing services, and home help services has been increasing, a comparative study in four Nordic countries in the mid-1980s showed that the amount of sheltered houses for the aged is in fact relatively low in Finland. It was also observed that home nursing and home help services are organized principally on weekdays and during the daytime and that these services were available not only to those needing help due to their disabilities (Jansson et al., 1987). Therefore, a reallocation of open care services for the elderly has been stressed during the past five years.

ELDER ABUSE

The "Discovery" of Elder Abuse

Family violence in younger and middle-aged families, and mainly physical abuse against wives and children, was discovered in Finland during the latter half of the 1970s. Experiments to help the victims of family violence were launched in the 1970s. One of the most active voluntary organizations in starting up these projects was the Federation of mother-child homes and shelters. In 1979, the Federation launched a three-year project, in four Finnish towns, to help both the victims of family violence and the abusers themselves. Abused persons were taken into the Federation's shelters, whose personnel tried to help victims by cooperating with the families, police, social welfare staff, health care personnel, and deacons and deaconesses (Heinänen, 1986).

During the project, the personnel at the shelters met all sorts of abused persons; not only abused young wives with their children, but also husbands and elderly persons seeking help. Between 3 and 6 percent of the clients seeking help were 65 years or over. Neither staff's training, which was intended for helping younger families with children, nor the shelter's facilities had been designed for elderly clients. The discovery of elder abuse and the difficulties in helping abused elders in the shelters inspired wide debate about the problem in Finland (Heinänen, 1986).

An article published by the Federation of mother-child homes and shelters in 1983, about elder abuse in Finland is one of the earliest papers on the problem. In 1985 the Federation started a major project to help the abused elderly. The project consisted of efforts to support the families of abused elderly, to illustrate the extent and types of the problem, to find explanations for it, to inform people about the problem, and to establish preventive measures (Heinänen, 1986). The academic community began to show a more serious interest in the problem in the latter half of the 1980s, when two major epidemiological studies were carried out on the extent and types of elder abuse (Kivelä, 1993a; Virjo & Kivelä, 1993).

The bulk of research into elder abuse during the 1980s was carried out in the U.S. Finnish researchers were very much influenced by the North American literature, as well as by Norwegian projects and experiences. The shelter staff and the researchers engaged in the Finnish project actively sought cooperation with experts in other Nordic countries, and the first Nordic seminar (with an expert from the U.S. about elder abuse) was held in 1986. More intensive cooperation between Nordic experts started in 1988; the aim was to explain and describe the extent of the problem in the Nordic countries, to synthesize the information collected in different Nordic projects, to inform the public in Finland, and to make suggestions for the prevention of problems and for helping the abused elderly in Finland.

The Extent and Risk of Elder Abuse

As was mentioned, there were two major epidemiological studies on elder abuse in Finland during the latter half of the 1980s. The material of the first study consisted of the population aged 65 years or over (N = 1225) in a semi-industrialized town in middle-western

Finland. The material of the second project consisted of the population aged 75 years or over living either in a semi-industrialized municipality or in a rural municipality in southern Finland (N = 871). The self-report data were collected by interviews, and the occurrence of abuse was defined by the elderly themselves (Kivelä, 1993a; Virjo & Kivelä, 1993).

Neither of these studies was exclusively concerned with the problems of elder abuse. The first aimed to describe and analyze depressive disorders in old age, while the second described the use of social and health care services among the elderly. Structured questions related to abuse were asked towards the end of the interviews. The subjects of both these studies are representative of the aged Finnish population living in rural or semi-industrialized areas. The results give the prevalence figures for elder abuse as reported by the elderly participants themselves; only a few in-depth interviews have been carried out to study abuse cases in more detail. It may be suggested that neglect to provide care is underestimated in these figures, because people with severe disabilities or dementia could not participate in the interviews (Kivelä et al., 1993; Virjo & Kivelä, 1993).

The results of the first study showed that 3.3 percent of men and 8.8 percent of women aged 65 years or over had been abused after the age of retirement, i.e., after the age of 60-65 years. The corresponding figures from the second study for the population aged 75 years or over were 7.7 percent for men and 8.3 percent for women (Kivelä et al., 1993; Virjo & Kivelä, 1993). In addition to abuse by family members, the above figures also include abuse by other relatives, friends, or strangers and abuse in institutions. When only abuse by spouse or child was taken into account, the prevalence rate was 1.0 percent for men and 5.3 percent for women aged 65 years or over. The prevalence rate of abuse by spouse, child, or relative was 2.5 percent for men and 7.0 percent for women (Kivelä et al., 1993).

There is no doubt that the elderly in Finland fall victim to both family violence and violence by strangers. Types and cases of family violence have been explored in greater depth in the descriptive studies and intervention programs by the Federation of mother-child homes and shelters, which have been only concerned with family violence. Finnish researchers have shown less interest in cases and types of neglect, sexual abuse, and in violence by strangers.

The most typical cases of family violence described in the Finnish literature include elderly women abused by their husbands (physical and mental abuse), elderly women abused by their sons (physical, mental, and economic abuse), elderly women or men abused by their daughters or sons (mainly economic and psychological abuse), elderly men abused by their wives (physical and mental abuse), and elderly men abused by their brothers (physical, mental, and economic abuse). In many cases the abuser has been under the influence of alcohol (Korhonen, 1992). In many families there is a history of decades of spousal abuse; namely, women abused by their husbands. The typical pattern is one where the husband gets heavily drunk once to four times a month and beats his wife (or abuses her in other, non-physical ways). In some cases the abuse started only after the husband fell ill and became disabled. In these cases, abuse may occur even when the husband has not been drinking (Korhonen, 1992).

One particular risk group for family violence is represented by elderly women, usually widowed, who live together with their unmarried or divorced son. The son has either never married (and has moved from home or worked outside the home) or he has married (and has moved from home and worked outside home) but divorced and moved back to live with his old mother. In either case, the son usually has an alcohol problem. He spends his mothers's money, gets drunk, and physically and mentally abuses her (Korhonen, 1992). There are also descriptions of family violence where elderly people repeatedly lose their money to young granddaughters, grandsons, or middle-aged daughters or sons. Mental abuse is very common in these cases (Korhonen, 1992).

Descriptions of family violence, in which the husband is being abused by the wife, can be divided into two groups: first, mental abuse that has continued for decades and second, mental and physical abuse that has started after the husband's illness and disability. In most cases, abuse by women also takes place under the influence of alcohol (Korhonen, 1992).

Elderly men living together with a brother constitute another potential risk group for abuse. Typically, the abuser has first lived with his wife and gone to work, but then divorced and lost his job (because of drinking) and has moved in with his brother. The abused brother has never had a family of his own, he has worked outside home, retired, and has no problems with alcohol. When under the influence, the brother abuses him both physically, mentally, and economically (Kivelä, 1993a).

Family violence is associated with depression and lack of intimate friends for both elderly Finnish men and women. Among depressed persons, family violence has usually continued for years (or even for decades) and may be a predisposing factor to depression (Kivelä, 1993a). Descriptions of elder abuse outside families include cases of physical abuse against an elderly man by a drunken stranger, economic abuse against an elderly person by a stranger visiting the home, and physical and economic abuse against an elderly person by a stranger in the street. In interviews, the elderly themselves have frequently stressed the problem of combined mental and economic violence by middle-aged strangers selling religious ideas door to door, trying to encourage them to join the religious movement or association, to give them money, or to buy books (Virjo & Kivelä, 1993). However, abuse outside families, caregiving neglect, and sexual abuse (either by a family member or by some other person) have all received less attention in research.

Abused elderly persons are visited by home nursing and home help personnel more often than the elderly who have not experienced family violence or violence by strangers. One possible explanation is that abused elders ask for help more often. It is also possible that the home helpers or nurses visiting the elderly person notice something is wrong, even though they see no immediate evidence of abuse and, therefore, decide to visit the patient more frequently (Virjo & Kivelä, 1993).

Explaining the Causes of Elder Abuse

Finnish researchers have found a close connection between elder abuse, use of alcohol, occurrence of depression (or other health problems), occurrence of social problems, and frequent use of home nursing and home help services. However, there have been no systematic efforts to develop a theory to explain the causes of elder abuse; instead, the theories employed in the Finnish literature and practical work have been imported from abroad. Included among the theories discussed in the Finnish literature are those that (1) focus on the individual problems of the abuser; (2) focus on physical and mental impairment of an older adult; (3) emphasize the efforts of stress on the caregiver; (4) deal with the influence of family members who solve problems by means of violence; (5) focus on the effects of a society (which cast older adults in the role of nonpersons through ageism, sexism, and destructive attitudes towards the disabled); and (6) advance biochemical and genetic hypotheses about the origin of family violence.

The Federation of mother-child homes and shelters in Finland has set up its shelters for abused people on the basis of the assumption that family violence is a problem that involves the entire family. The aim has been to help both the victim and the abuser. Feminist theories that family violence is a result of sexism and lack of gender equality have received less attention in Finland, especially among social and health care workers for the elderly (Korhonen, 1992).

Efforts to Prevent, Detect, and Intervene in Elder Abuse

The most serious efforts to identify the problem of elder abuse in Finland have been undertaken by the Federation of mother-child homes and shelters, as well as a small group of researchers. These people have written about the problem, organized seminars to discuss the problem, and started Nordic cooperation to develop prevention and intervention programs. They have also given lectures on the subject in continuing education courses arranged for workers providing public social and health care to the elderly. The descriptions of individual cases of abuse by the participants in these seminars and courses are consistent with the findings of the researchers and with the experiences of the personnel from the Federation of mother-child homes and shelters. Social and health care workers have drawn special attention to the difficulties of helping abused elderly persons. The major problems are the lack of knowledge about the causes of elder abuse, the practical difficulties of intervention, and the lack of close cooperation between social welfare, health care, and police authorities.

The public sector and government in Finland have not shown a very active interest in the detection, prevention, and intervention of elder abuse. In fact, no public programs have been started, nor have any public research grants been issued. Nordic cooperation has been supported by the Nordic Council of Ministers. The information effort, so far, has concentrated on professional social and health care staff, whereas the information needs of the general public have been largely neglected. The press has only carried stories of individual cases of elderly persons either physically or economically abused by strangers in the street or in their homes. The media in Finland have made no serious effort to inform the general public about the problem, to describe existing safeguards, or to come forward with suggestions for better prevention.

There has been only one prevention and intervention program; this was organized by the Federation of mother-child homes and shelters in three Finnish towns from 1985 to 1987. In Turku, the program consisted of collecting information about the prevalence and types of elder abuse in the town. Staff working in the shelters in public social and health care or in the welfare services organized by the church, voluntary associations, and the police were trained; efforts were made to organize an open-care team to help abused elderly people (Korhonen, 1992).

In Helsinki and Kotka, the program aimed to intensify cooperation between the staff of shelters and welfare services organized by the church and the police. In addition, training courses for the personnel were arranged. Abused elderly in seriously-ill health were referred to nursing homes cooperating with the shelters (Korhonen, 1992). The people engaged in this program have arranged seminars and cooperated with local newspapers and radio to help inform the general public and the elderly themselves about the problem and how to get help. A family-oriented approach has been stressed, and both abused women and men (and their abusers) have been helped (Korhonen, 1992).

In practice, the interventions have included opportunities for elderly persons abused by their spouse or child to rest for a few days in the shelter or in a nursing home. Attempts to clear up the difficult situation at home take into account the needs of both the abused person and the abuser. Cooperation with the public social welfare and health care sectors and other social welfare organizations has also been stressed. The victim and the abuser have been given the opportunity to discuss their situation with the shelter or nursing home staff, even months after the acute period (Korhonen, 1992).

A new voluntary organization called the Federation of Shelters for the Finnish Elderly has been registered in 1989. The aims of this organization are to inform the general public (and political decision-makers) about elder abuse, to follow up international and national studies and intervention programs, and to set up support groups for abused elderly. The organization has arranged a telephone information service for the elderly, the general public, and social and health care personnel (Korhonen, 1992).

In addition to an evaluation of the program organized by the Federation of mother-child homes and shelters, several papers have been published on the types of family violence against Finnish elderly persons. There are also case reports on the work that has been done to help these people. These reports are mainly directed to the personnel of the public social and health care system, the aim being to develop their skills and knowledge of detection, prevention, and intervention. Although the actual program closed down in 1987, the Federation's shelters continue to provide help for abused elderly and their abusers in the future. Nevertheless, it remains an urgent priority to introduce such services in the public sector, too (Korhonen, 1992).

The findings from the two epidemiological studies about elder abuse in Finland have now been analyzed, and the reports are currently in press. The researchers involved in these studies have been active in giving lectures on how the problem of elder abuse can be prevented and how the victims can be helped.

FUTURE PROJECTIONS

Both the public and private economy in Finland are suffering from one of the deepest recessions in the country's history. Unemployment rates have climbed to unprecedented levels, particularly in the age group 18-25 years. Although social security for the individual citizen in Finland is much better than in many other industrialized countries and although all unemployed people are entitled to benefits, those who have been unemployed for periods of time are quite poor. The custom in today's generation of old people has been to save money, which means there are many people who own farms or flats or who (otherwise) have money. The amount of pension paid to elderly people varies, but it may be quite considerable compared with unemployment benefits. If the current recession in Finland continues, there is an obvious risk that we will see more economic exploitation against the elderly in families. This is confirmed by the individual cases reported by social and health care workers. Unemployment also spills over into increased burglaries; the statistics show that the figures have been rising for the past two to three years. The elderly are, of course, particularly vulnerable victims.

Another trend with serious consequences is the continued reduction of services by the municipalities which will continue to reduce their services during the next few years. Due to ageism and negative attitudes towards the elderly, it is likely that the elderly will be most affected by these cuts. There is currently a strong tendency towards the privatization of social and health care services. Private home nursing and home help services in a country like Finland, that has a large area but a low population density, are expensive for their users, even if they are subsidized by the state. If the elderly do not have the money to purchase these services, the private sector will not be interested in providing them. The shortages of public home care services and the non-availability of reasonably priced private services may lead to a lack of concrete and affective support by the formal care system. The disabled elderly themselves or the families taking care of them may not get enough support. Exhausted family members may abuse their elderly.

The current economic recession and high unemployment may lead to the emergence of new demands in society. Public opinion may change, and employed people with low incomes may have to look after their elderly parents themselves. Even highly-educated women may have to give up their jobs to unemployed men and stay at home to care for their elderly parents. These pressing demands, together with the lack of public services, may increase the amount of violence against the elderly. The reduction of staff levels in the public social and health care sectors may also give rise to exhaustion and burn-out. Neglect and abuse by professionals, even in institutions, may become an increasingly serious problem. In short then, there is reason to believe that elder abuse will increase in the future. How can Finnish society prevent this from happening? Voluntary organizations working with the elderly, and especially with abused elderly, as well as researchers in this field, should try to encourage more active debate on this issue, its prevalence, prevention, and intervention. The prevention and intervention of elder abuse can be organized by public social and health care services in cooperation with voluntary organizations, the welfare services organized by the church, and the police. Further education courses for workers engaged in the care of the elderly should be offered so that abused elders can get more competent help.

Researchers must continue to monitor the prevalence and types of elder abuse in Finland. As well as doing epidemiological studies, researchers must follow-up by interviewing workers in public and voluntary agencies serving the elderly. Preventive programs and interventions must be monitored and evaluated. Researchers must carefully follow-up not only Nordic, but also international, studies and programs on this topic and try to transfer the international experiences to practical work in Finland.

REFERENCES

Heinänen, A. (ed.) (1986). Banhus ja perheväkivalta. Ensi Kotien Liiton julkaisu nro 8. Ensi Kotien Liitto, Helsinki 1986. (The elderly and family violence. Report of the Federation of mother-child homes and shelters. N: 0 8. Helsinki 1986).

Jansson, T., Wallberg, E., Albrektson, K. (1987). Ädreomsorg i Norden. (Care of the elderly in Nordic Countries. Costs, quality, administration. KRON-project. Stockholm 1987).

Kivelä, S-L. (1983a) Övergrepp mot äldre i Finland–en allmänbild. In: Övergrepp mot äldre i Norden. Mordiska Ministerrådets rapport 1993a. (Elder abuse in Finland–An overview. In: Elder abuse in Nordic Countries. Report of Nordic Council or Ministers. (In press.)

Kivelä, S-L. (1993b). The Finnish elderly and their families. Manuscript.

Kivelä, S-L, Köngäs-Saviaro, P, Kesti, E, Pahkala ,K, Ijäs, M-L. (1993). Abuse in old age–Epidemiological data from Finland. Journal of Elder Abuse & Neglect, 4 (3), 1-18.

Korhonen, L. (ed.) (1987). Vanhus perheväkivallan kohteena. Ensi Kotien Liiton

raporttisarja nro 1, Helsinki 1987. (Family violence against the elderly. Report of the Federation of mother-child homes and shelters. N:0 1. Helsinki 1987).
Korhonen, L. Levoton vanhuus, Ensi- ja turvakotien liiton raportti nor 9. ensi- ja turvakotien liiktto, Helsink i 1992. (Korhonen L. Abuse in old age. Report of the federation of mother-child homes and shelters. N:0 9. Helsinki 1992).
Virjo, I. & Kivelä, S-L. Övergrepp mot äldre i Finland–erfarenheter från personer 75 å och äldre. In: Övergrepp mot äldre i Norden. Nordiska Ministersrådets rapport 1993. (Elder abuse in Finland–Experiences as told by persons aged 75 years or older. In: Elder abuse in Nordic countries. Report of Nordic Council of Ministers 1993). (In press.)
Statistics Finland. Statistical yearbook of Finland 1992. Helsinki 1992.

Chapter 4

Mistreatment of the Elderly in Greece

Eleni N. Pitsiou-Darrough, PhD
C. D. Spinellis, JD, PhD

While elder mistreatment is not a new phenomenon, there is little awareness in contemporary Greek society of the problem or the degree of its existence. An examination of literary and historical sources reveals that elder abuse has not emerged as a result of high levels of "modernization," "industrialization," or because of the "breakdown of the family." Old age was feared and mourned by the life-loving Greeks in ancient times. It seems that nothing has changed with the passage of time. Greek history reveals clear cases of selfish carelessness or coarse insolence toward the old. Athenian history, for example, offers several instances of children taking over their parents' property without proof of incapacity in the elders, even though Athenian law required that sons must support their infirm or aged parents. Also, public opinion, which always creates more fear than the law, decrees modesty and respect in the behavior of the young toward the old.

Disputes over whether the incidence and prevalence of elder mistreatment are greater now than in the past should not obstruct

Eleni N. Pitsiou-Darrough is Professor, Sociology-Gerontology, Department of Sociology, California State University, Los Angeles, and C. D. Spinellis is Associate Professor, Section of Criminal Law and Criminology, Faculty of Law, University of Athens, 57 Solonos Strt GR-10679 Athens Greece.

[Haworth co-indexing entry note]: "Mistreatment of the Elderly in Greece." Pitsiou-Darrough, Eleni N., and C.D. Spinellis. Co-published simultaneously in the *Journal of Elder Abuse & Neglect* (The Haworth Press, Inc.) Vol. 6, No. 3/4, 1995, pp. 45-64; and: *Elder Abuse: International and Cross-Cultural Perspectives* (ed: Jordan I. Kosberg, and Juanita L. Garcia) The Haworth Press, Inc., 1995, pp. 45-64. Multiple copies of this article/chapter may be purchased from The Haworth Document Delivery Center [1-800-3-HAWORTH; 9:00 a.m. - 5:00 p.m. (EST)].

efforts to examine this social problem. One must acknowledge its existence, examine it, and try to find a solution while it is still amenable to control. As Greece entered its modern era, there were some striking shifts in cultural values and expectations about filial responsibilities. Some academicians have speculated that the changing demographic characteristics of the population will have a negative impact both on family relationships and on the incidence and prevalence of abuse and neglect among the elderly.

Presently, as the number and the proportion of older Greeks expand, their health care needs present a new challenge to Greek society. Paradoxically, as science extends life, socially supported services for the elderly decline and the demands on their families increase. Most of the care given to the elderly in Greece today is provided by the informal care system, including spouses, children, neighbors, relatives, and friends. Also, the rapid growth of the old-old population, with its medical and economic needs, represents a new predicament for many families.

This chapter addresses several questions about elder mistreatment. What are the changes in the contemporary Greek family? How prevalent is elder abuse, who are the abused, and who are the abusers? What protections are given to the elderly in the legal system and in social policy?

DEMOGRAPHIC CHARACTERISTICS

This section will present information on the major demographic characteristics of the older people with particular emphasis on the effects of industrialization and urbanization on the lives of the elderly. To understand the status and the treatment of the old in modern Greek society, the changes that have taken place in the Greek family structure will be related to the changes in the demographic characteristics of the Greek population. As will be shown, physical dependency of the elderly is one of the most important risk factors for mistreatment.

The percentage of older persons in the total population is constantly increasing. In 1961 persons over the age of 60 numbered 1,023,500 (12.2%), their numbers increased to 1,397,000 in 1971 (15.9%) and reached 1,649,455 (16.9%) by 1981. Also, there is a lower ratio of males to females for persons 60 years of age and over (15.3 and 18.3%, respectively) (Spinellis & Pitsiou-Darrough, 1991a).

Similarly, it has been estimated that by the year 2000 the proportion of persons 65 years of age and over will reach 20 percent, making Greece a country with one of the oldest populations in Europe. Presently, Greece has the highest proportion of older people among the Balkan countries. In the mid-1980s, life expectancy of the old-old (75 years and older) was listed as 8.8 years for men and 10.3 years for women and is constantly increasing. The distribution of the Greek population is heavily weighted to the two major urban centers which have almost half of Greece's population. Athens, the capital of Greece, has approximately four million persons, while Salonica, in Northern Greece, has about one million (Spinellis & Pitsiou-Darrough, 1991).

Considerable differences exist in the number of elderly individuals who live in urban centers in contrast to rural areas. There is a constant increase in the urban population at the expense of the rural population. The proportion of people over the age of 60 who live in urban inner city areas are in neighborhoods that are already overpopulated, and living conditions in these neighborhoods are very difficult for many older people. In 1961, only 40.2 percent of the elderly were living in urban centers; by 1971 the proportion of elderly in urban areas increased to 46.1 percent and by 1981 approximately half (49.0%) of the elderly were living in urban areas. A study conducted by the Center of Planning and Economic Research revealed that over one-fourth of the households in urban areas (29.7%), in which the head of the household was 60 years of age or older, were living in small two room houses (Kanelopoulos, 1984).

In 1981, persons 60 years of age and older comprised 16.9 percent of the population and those over the age of 65 made up 13 percent. However, they averaged more hospital days than any other age group and they occupied 40 percent of all hospital beds (Spinellis & Pitsiou-Darrough, 1991a). It has been estimated that 4,500 older individuals enter a hospital due to a hip fracture every year (Georgiathis, 1987). The increase in life expectancy has resulted in a larger proportion of elderly with mental problems, limited mobility, depression, cognitive impairment, or other chronic illnesses (Fotaki, 1983).

Of the over 65 age group, 64.3 percent are married. However, the widening gap in survival rates between the sexes creates a situation in which a much higher percentage of males (88.1%) than females (45.2%) are currently married. For those over the age of 80, only 8.6 percent of the women and 62.5 percent of the men are married. Almost six percent of the males are widowers, while 28.2 percent of the women are widows, and there are fewer never married men (1.7%) than single never married women (2.6%).

The living arrangements of the elderly are related to their marital status. Ninety percent of the married men 60 years of age and over are heads of their household, while this is true for only 37.4 percent of the widowed or divorced men. Similarly, 85.1 percent of married women are married to the head of the household. A variety of other arrangements, however, are also possible. For example, 17 percent of never married men live in a household headed by a brother, and 27 percent of never married women live in a household headed by a sister. At the beginning of the 1980s, 25 percent of 60-64 year olds and 35 percent of those aged 85-89 lived in households containing four or more other people.

In the early 1980s, the National Statistical Service of Greece (1982) conducted a study which revealed that 4.7 percent of those over 65 lived alone in one-person households; of those living alone, 18 percent were men and 82 percent were women (Loizos, 1986). The proportion of old people living alone has grown in recent years but is still very low in comparison to other countries. The typical pattern continues: "The Greek elderly population lives in its own household as long as both spouses are alive. When one of them dies the other goes to live with one of their children, preferably their son" (Loizos 1986: 10).

DISCOVERING ELDER ABUSE

In the 1980s, when family violence as well as elder abuse and neglect became major issues, both at popular and scientific levels, many European countries attempted to identify the incidence and prevalence of elder abuse. In 1987 the lack of information on this issue and the need to collect appropriate data to determine its existence and extent became apparent.

During that year, the Council of Europe organized a colloquium on family violence. The Greek representatives to the colloquium had limited knowledge of the prevalence of elder abuse or neglect in Greece. Before the meeting, the Greek Ministry of Health and Social Welfare, Department of Aging, conducted an inquiry to estimate the prevalence of elder abuse. Specifically, the Department of Aging requested information on elder abuse or neglect from some major hospitals in the greater Athens area. The social service department of the Principal Orthopedic hospital in Athens (KAT) gathered very significant data. They reported that physical violence against elderly people was very limited. Using a representative method of data collection, they examined the admittance records and the emergency department books to find the number of patients who were treated for an injury during the months of May through August 1987. The results indicated that out of 16, 000 patients who were brought to the hospital for different injuries, only 33 cases were diagnosed as beatings (equal to 0.2%). Of the 33 cases, only six (18.2%) were persons 65 years of age and older.

Similarly, reports from four general hospitals in the greater Athens area revealed few physical abuse or assault cases against elderly people. The Social Service Departments of these hospitals reported that they treated, on average, six cases of physical abuse or assault per month. However, all hospitals implied that the major problem was that of neglect or abandonment, not of physical abuse. Although this inquiry did not prove elder abuse to be a major problem in Greece, it showed that elderly persons who become victims of abuse or neglect are not an unknown phenomenon in Greek society.

No doubt, major hospitals are important points of data-gathering for issues such as abuse and neglect, but the data gathered by the Department of Aging was limited in its generalizability because of the small, nonrandom sample of hospitals. Also, most of the information gathered by the hospitals was incomplete. For example, sometimes cases of assault or violence were placed under the category "accident." Another issue is the lack of information on the abuser. When information on the abuser was not available, it was impossible to determine if the abuse was intrafamily abuse or was external to the family.

At the colloquium mentioned above, only three countries (England, Norway and Finland) reported research activities in the field of elder abuse. In response, the Council of Europe recommended that member governments investigate the problem.

In sum, the limited information on elder abuse and neglect in Greece, the need to establish national policy on the issue of victimization of the elderly, and the need to inform different international organizations, required a more extensive and well-organized study. In December 1987, the Department of Penal Law of the University of Athens Law School was awarded a grant by the Department of Aging to study the problem of elder abuse and neglect. For the next two years they conducted the first large scale study of elder mistreatment in Greece. A discussion of some of the results of this study follows. The full results can be found in Spinellis and Pitsiou-Darrough (1991a; 1991b).

THE NATURE AND EXTENT OF ELDER ABUSE

As noted above, the impetus for the study of elder abuse in Greece came from the Council of Europe. This study was an attempt to determine the extent and etiology of violence and the nature of abuse and neglect as a social, medical, and legal problem. The samples included older adults age 60 or older who lived at home, alone or with other family members. Institutional abuse was excluded.

There were several research questions that guided the study. First, what was the demographic profile of the victims of abuse? Second, what were the differences in the characteristics of abused and non-abused elders? Third, what forms of abuse were the most common forms of victimization? Fourth, what was the cost of abuse to the family and society? Finally, was there any evidence of other factors, such as physical, mental, or other limitations, that might increase the vulnerability of an elderly person to abuse?

Research Design and Sample

A purposive comparative design was used to conduct the study because this was the first project on elder abuse in Greece and the availability of any information on the subject was very limited. Ten KAPH centers (Open Care Centers for the elderly) from the county of Attica, the largest county in Greece where one-third of Greeks live, were randomly selected out of a list of 71 centers in operation in 1988. In each center, the interviewer responsible for collecting the data was given specific instructions for the selection of a random number of respondents. Also, a random sub-sample of elderly respondents was selected from the same ten communities from which the KAPH samples were selected. This group of subjects was included in the study as a control group.

Further, the books of the police stations of the ten communities were examined to determine if any crimes had been committed against persons over the age of 60 during a six-month period (October 1988 through February 1989). Also, in order to assess the level of abuse in other areas of Greece, an investigation of service providers was included in the study. All the KAPH centers and all the state hospitals of Greece were included in this sub-sample. One hundred and forty hospitals (140) and 211 KAPH centers were contacted and asked to participate in the study. The collection of data from professionals was included in order to compare the general characteristics of abused elders in the district of Attica with those of other abused victims in other parts of the country.

Data Collection

The primary data were collected during a nine month period from October 1988 through June 1989. Letters were sent to all the service providers of the KAPH centers and the state hospitals of Greece, requesting their cooperation. Consent to cooperate from qualifying respondents was obtained by the interviewers during the initial contact and during that time the nature and purpose of the study was explained. In assessing whether a qualifying respondent should be interviewed, consideration was given to the individual's pathology. A set of questions was included in the interview instrument in an attempt to define the capability of the respondent to take part in the study. Trained interviewers conducted the interviews at the different settings.

Completion Rate

Five hundred and six elderly persons (506) were interviewed at the ten KAPH centers. Two-hundred and fifty-one (251) respondents were included in the control group. In each community, between 24 to 26 older individuals were interviewed at home. The care providers returned 131 completed questionnaires. Reports of elder abuse came from 21 hospitals and 75 KAPH centers.

Interview Instruments

Interview schedules were developed specifically for this study. One was designed for the elderly subjects from the KAPH centers and for the control group. A different one was designed for the service providers, administrators, and/or social workers. The interview schedules were written in clear simple language and presented in an easily administered format. An attempt was made to develop interview schedules that would be easily understood by respondents of different intellectual and educational levels. An attempt was also made to include several open-ended questions so that respondents could elaborate when they wished. Given the difficulty involved in discussing topics such as abuse, an assumption was made that respondents would require both structured and unstructured opportunities to do so.

The variables for which information was sought were basic demographic characteristics, information regarding individual abuse or abuse of another person in the last few days, as well as information about the abuser and the place of abuse. An effort was also made to determine the subject's perception of the reason for the abuse. Information also was sought about different types of abuse that the subject might have suffered in the past 12 months and any health problem or injury that resulted from this abuse. Additional questions obtained information regarding days of hospitalization or medical treatment received by the abused elder for each type of abuse he or she experienced in the last 12 months. The last section included questions pertaining to the subject's lifestyle and family structure and information on specific characteristics that could reduce the older person's capacity to resist or retaliate against abuse occurrence. All sections included questions regarding abuse of another person.

Service-Provider Interview Schedule

Information was requested regarding both the care provider and the victim. Data on the care provider included personal and professional work experience and knowledge regarding elder abuse. The second part consisted of a separate schedule that focused on the most observable characteristics of the abused person and the abuser, data likely to be available in case records of the surveyed services.

Operational Definitions

This study examined two major areas of mistreatment: (a) active mistreatment and (b) passive mistreatment. Active mistreatment included intentional harm or abuse, such as physical, psychological, and legal, against an elder. Notably, physical abuse was defined as any form of bodily violence and was measured by a series of items that covered a range of violent behaviors, from being pushed or beaten to being sexually abused. Psychological abuse was defined as mental anguish and was operationalized using a single item regarding verbal abuse or insults. Legal abuse was defined as material exploitation and misuse or theft of an elder's money or other assets and was measured with a single question. Passive mistreatment implied unintentional harm, such as neglect and abandonment, against an elder. Neglect (physical, psychological or environmental) was measured by a series of items designed to determine if the older person needed help with daily living activities and help was withheld.

Characteristics of Respondents

The sample was quite similar demographically to both the over 60 population of the greater Athens area and Greece. In all, 55 percent of the sample were female and 98 percent were Christian Orthodox. Almost half of the KAPH respondents (44% in a sample of 506 respondents) and a little over half of the control group (56% in a sample of 251 respondents) were married and living with their spouse; over one-third of the control group and 42 percent of the KAPH subjects were widowed; and a small number, between 4 and 7 percent, was never married or divorced. In both samples, over 60 percent of the respondents were living in single family homes and smaller numbers, between 28 to 39 percent were living in apartments. The majority, 71 percent from the KAPH sample and 80 percent from the control group, were living with their spouse and children. The fact that 27 percent of respondents from the KAPH sample and only 19 percent from the control group were living alone, might indicate that the KAPH centers fulfill a major need of many individuals for companionship.

Most subjects indicated that they received a pension (83% from the KAPH sample and 80% from the control group), and a small number (15%) reported receiving income from other sources, such as rent or help from their children. One-third of the subjects from the first group and one-half from the second stated that their income was not enough to meet their daily needs. There were only minor differences in the educational level of the two samples. Over one-third (37%) of the respondents had graduated from elementary school and one-third (33%) had less than six years of schooling. Smaller numbers had finished high school (12%) and 17 percent had some post-secondary education. Finally, almost half of the subjects from both groups stated that their health was either "good" or "very good" and a little over one-third indicated that their health was "very poor."

Degree and Type of Mistreatment of Elderly People in Greece

The findings clearly point out that mistreatment of the elderly is not an unknown phenomenon in Greece (Table 1). Of the 757 respondents, a total of 117 had suffered some type of abuse, either a few days before the interview took place or within the previous year. In addition, 109 respondents knew of at least one case of elder abuse. They did not report any major criminal violence against them, and a small number of those reporting physical abuse needed hospitalization. The most frequently-cited abuse reported by both samples was verbal abuse, such as insults. However, on the average six to ten respondents had been subjected to some type of physical abuse or neglect. The service providers reported 131 cases of elder abuse, including 81 cases of physical abuse and 106 cases of neglect. One of the most significant findings of this survey was the multiple abuses suffered by the elderly. Twenty-two elderly stated that they endured more than three types of abuse, ten elderly had suffered between five and eleven types, and thirteen had been subjected to two types. The rest mentioned only one type of abuse.

The present study could not determine if any elderly victims had

TABLE 1. Abuse Occurring in the Previous Year by Sex of Respondent.

ABUSE	KAPH SAMPLE				CONTROL SAMPLE				SERVICE PROVIDERS' REPORT			
	Male		Female		Male		Female		Male		Female	
	N	%	N	%	N	%	N	%	N	%	N	%
Physical Abuse	9	29	11	21	2	18	3	15	31	36	50	30
Material Abuse	7	23	9	17	3	27	6	30	5	6	18	11
Psychological Abuse	9	29	19	37	6	55	6	30	7	8	33	20
Neglect	6	19	13	25	0	0	5	25	43	50	63	38
TOTAL ABUSE	31	100	52	100	11	100	20	100	86	100	164	100

Source: Spinellis & Pitsiou-Darrough, 1991a, 1991b.

died as a result of abuse. Such cases, although rare, have been reported by the press. For example: "A. S., a 72 year-old woman, was found dead yesterday afternoon, with multiple wounds on her head, in her home, in the village of Kilia Kalavryton. The police are investigating the crime."

Characteristics of Abused Respondents

Women were victimized more often than men, and individuals under the age of 70 suffered more abuse than persons over 70. Lower percentages of mistreated and neglected elderly were found among those individuals who were living alone, and the highest number of neglected individuals was reported by the service providers. Most abused elderly (67%) lived with a relative and in many cases (51% among the KAPH respondents and only 16% from the control group) the abuser was a family member. Similar findings were reported by the service providers.

Most mistreated subjects from both samples were single, divorced or widowed (56%). The majority of the abused elders from both groups had active visiting patterns, although they maintained low levels of telephone contact and organizational participation. The service providers reported that only 12 percent of the abused elders were married while the majority (88%) were single, divorced, or widowed. They also reported that most of the elderly lived alone (63%), a fact that explains the higher rate of passive neglect reported for these subjects.

Of major concern is the fact that such a large number of KAPH members indicated that they had suffered from some type of abuse. One possible explanation is that some types of abuse are acceptable to some extent in Greek society and therefore are not recognized or defined as abuse by most individuals. It is also possible that since the KAPH respondents were interviewed by social workers of the KAPH centers who had an established level of contact with them, the older people might have felt more comfortable talking to them.

Most abused respondents (55% from the KAPH sample and 43% from the control group) stated that their health status was not very good. Despite the fact that such a large number of abused respondents perceived their health as poor, the conclusion cannot be reached that they were abused due to their physical condition. At this point it is only speculation that their health status influenced their ability to resist abuse. Since the sample did not include subjects who were mentally impaired, it is not known whether impaired mental and physical functioning, when present in the same individual, might lead to higher levels of mistreatment. The majority of the abused respondents, however, had a very poor self-concept and very low levels of life satisfaction. Recognizing their predicament and unable to find a solution to their problem, these abused elders continue to live in unhealthy environments.

Relationship of Abuser to the Abused

In 51 percent of the citings in the KAPH sample, the abuser was a relative, most often a spouse or a child. Nonrelatives accounted for 34 percent of abusing persons. Fifteen percent of the victims blamed themselves for their condition. In the control group, 16 percent of the respondents stated that the abusing person was a relative and 16 percent indicated that the abusing person was a nonrelative, friend, or neighbor; additionally, 60 percent did not know their abuser. The service providers reported that 38 percent of the victims had been abused by a relative and 17% were cases of self-neglect.

Police Records of Abuse Reports

The records of the police departments in the same 10 communities where the KAPH centers were located were examined, for the same time period (September 1988 to February 1989), to determine the level of reporting of victimization on the part of the victim. The reports were compared to the percentage of abused elders from the KAPH centers and the control group interviews and to the ratio of men to women in the ten sampling areas and to the ratio of men to women in the national population. It can be seen in Table 2 that while more women than men reported different types of abuse in the personal interviews, more men than women were listed as victims of some type of abuse in the police records. However, most of the victims in the police records were identified as victims of theft or of other material abuse. Only four listings alluded to some type of verbal or physical abuse as a result of interpersonal mistreatment.

TABLE 2. Abused Victims from Different Sampling Units and Police Reports, Compared to the 60 and Older Population of the Sampling Areas and Greece.

SEX	KAPH GROUP Victims		CONTROL GROUP Victims		POLICE REPORTS Victims		POPULATION 60+ Sampling Areas	POPULATION 60+ National
	N	%	N	%	N	%	%	%
Male	33	9	12	5	35	54	44	45
Female	47	7	25	10	30	46	56	55
Total	80	16	37	15	65	100	100	100

Source: Spinellis & Pitsiou-Darrough, 1991a, 1991b.

These findings generate more questions than answers. Why do police records contain so few cases of elder abuse? Are elderly people under-reporting or is the lack of information in the police records the result of a police system that is not set up to intervene in cases of family violence? Is it more acceptable for a male to report a crime to the police or are there more male than female victims of material abuse?

LEGAL AND SOCIAL PROTECTION FOR VICTIMS OF ELDER ABUSE AND NEGLECT

Protection and the Legal System

The Greek social and legal systems currently offer limited protection to the elderly who become victims of abuse. Albeit, the Greek Criminal Code contains several provisions that implicitly or explicitly protect the elderly. An elderly victim, as can be surmised from the Code of Penal Procedure (C. P. P.), can file a complaint with the help of a legal representative against an abusing individual. Further, according to the C. P. P., elderly persons can give a deposition at home when " . . . sick or too old to appear in court to testify under oath and their testimony can be introduced as evidence in court . . ." (article 215, C. P. P). The Penal Code System, however, applies to those few extreme cases where there is intentional homicide or the offense is conceived and committed while in a state of psychological excitement, negligent homicide, failure to avert a danger to life, exposure to harm, or suicidal complicity (Articles, 299, 302, 307, 306, 301).

While the Penal Code contains provisions that protect the rights of minors against bodily ill-treatment, injury to health, sexual abuse, or against "one who for gain takes advantage of the carelessness or inexperience of a minor . . ." it does not provide for the elderly victims who because of diminished capacity, mental or physical, become victims of robbery, mainly of purse snatching, illicit appropriation, theft or even extortion, fraud, or sexual abuse or rape. Also, if older persons become victims of unlawful duress or threat and/or they are insulted (the most common crimes against elderly), it is necessary to file a complaint to resolve the issue. A baffling question arises when the person who committed the abuse against the elderly person is a relative. Would the victim be willing to start legal proceedings?

Protection and the Social System

Presently, there is no special system specifically designated to offer protection or psychological, legal, socioeconomic, or medical assistance to elderly victims of abuse or neglect in Greece. Under the existing structure, there are a number of services available to the elderly. First, public hospitals offer hospitalization and treatment to severe cases of abuse when they are brought to the hospitals. Although the public hospitals for the chronically disabled offer their services to all adults, not only to the elderly, they are able to provide help to some severe cases of abuse that result in permanent disability.

Second, the Centers of Open Care for the Elderly offer their help as well. Known as KAPH in Greece, they are public centers that were organized to offer opportunities for social participation and preventive medical care to the elderly in their communities. The goal of this system is to keep the elderly active and independent. The emphasis given here is in the utilization and transference of the cultural heritage the elderly possess and the rejection of the isolation, dependence, and institutionalization of the elderly. The first center opened, experimentally, in 1979 and by 1989, 250 centers were operating in the country, with 80 centers in the district of Attica. The KAPH centers are each staffed by a social worker, a visiting nurse, a physical therapist, an ergotherapist, home service assistants and a medical doctor.

Third, a temporary but inadequate solution to the problem of elder abuse can be found in the idea of public guest-houses for adults. These guest-houses are limited in number and were developed to temporarily house adults of all age groups during a critical period in their life. Older people, because of their special needs, can be accommodated in these houses only in exceptional circumstances.

More help is provided, however, to individuals who run the risk of abuse, under new provisions that were instituted by the government for the protection of the elderly. Some of the most important of these provisions are listed below:

a. In 1983 the privilege of lifelong housing was established under a program offered by the Department of Public Housing of the Department of Health, Welfare and Social Security for individuals over the age of 65. A more recent program, instituted in 1985, covers rental expenses by paying for the rent directly to the owner of the house for persons who do not have a home or who have no families or for couples who have no insurance and are over the age of 65.

b. A "Home Help" program, offered in collaboration between the local government and the Greek Red Cross, provides help to everybody but mainly older, isolated persons in need of assistance.

c. Special tax provisions, such as a tax reduction for old people, who are handicapped, blind or over the age of 67.

d. A special transportation pass that allows people over the age of 60 to use the buses, subways, and trains within Greece, as well as for travel abroad, under the "Rail Europe Senior," at reduced rates.

e. Summer camps for the members of the KAPH centers and for those individuals who are participating in the "home help" and "social tourism" programs.

f. Phone installation, without delay, in the homes of persons who live alone and are over the age of 75. Also, a private phone line is installed for an elderly person over the age of 80 living in the same house with other family members. (In Greece, often people have to wait for years to have a phone installed in their homes.)

CONCLUSIONS AND FUTURE PROJECTIONS

When all the data collected in Greece on the problem of elder abuse and neglect are reviewed, several important issues emerge for discussion. The general picture may lead to the conclusion that Greece does not face, at least at present, a grave problem of violence and mistreatment of its elderly citizens, since the major forms of abuse against elderly were those of the psychological type, specifically, verbal abuse. However, psychological abuse from the point of view of the victim could be as serious or even more important than physical abuse. It is important to note, also, that the study data (Spinellis & Pitsiou-Darrough, 1991a, 1991b) revealed that six out of ten respondents stated that they had suffered one or more acts of physical abuse within a 12 month period. A total of 117 elderly persons, from the KAPH sample and the control group, had been mistreated in the past twelve months. This translates into a rate of 154 mistreated elderly per 1000. These comparatively high levels of abuse among our respondents suggest that the present provisions for the protection of the elderly citizens are deficient. However, severe cases of abuse involving death or other major crimes against elderly were reported only by the mass media and received great publicity. Also, the data gathered from the police departments did not reveal any major crimes, specifically violence leading to the death of the victim.

Media coverage of neglect and abandonment focuses on the most sensational cases. The cases of abandonment and/or neglect, uncovered by the study on elder abuses in the greater Athens area samples, were very few in contrast to those cases reported to us by the service providers of the hospitals and KAPH centers of the other areas of Greece, as well as those reported by the Ministry of Health and Social Security, Department of Aging (1987). However, no matter how limited the number of cases might be, they do present a major hurdle to the already overcrowded public hospitals and an urgent need for a solution of this problem.

Although family violence might not present Greek society with a serious challenge, according to our data it is present in significant numbers. The abusers in 51 percent of the cases of abuse reported by the members of KAPH centers were family members. That is, one out of two respondents was abused by a relative, most often by a spouse or a child. Yet, the subjects of the control group and the reports received from the service providers revealed lower levels of family violence. Specifically, one-sixth of the control group subjects and a little over one-third of the cases reported by the service providers were intrafamily conflict cases. Older persons who were living with others were at higher risk for abuse compared to those living alone. Moreover, the fact that women tend to live with other family members may explain in part why the rate of intrafamily abuse of women is higher compared to that of men.

Given the fact that different forms of mistreatment against the elderly are present in the Greek society, the underlying sources of the problem should be addressed. Further research is needed in order to determine the social and economic costs of elder abuse. Solutions must be found and programs developed to alleviate the problem, not only because Greece needs to comply with the standards established by international organizations, but for two other very important reasons. Firstly, issues of this kind disrupt and change the balance of the Greek society, where the elderly are not only removed from major roles but are not even protected by their society during the later years of their life. Secondly, Greece, like many other European countries, is faced with major demographic changes that are dramatically influencing the distribution of the older population in the age structure. Specifically, the gap of those under the age of 15 and those over the age of 64 is getting smaller and smaller. This situation will create further problems for our society and our older citizens.

In conclusion, from the results of this study of elder abuse, the only study on this problem at present, it is probable that family relationships should be examined more closely and the traditional Greek family re-evaluated. Additional information is needed based on measures used in other more technologically advanced societies, at the same time keeping in mind that removing the elderly from their families and placing them in institutions should always be the last resort, the *ultimum refugium.*

REFERENCES

Conseil de l'Europe. (1987). Colloque au sein de la famille-mesures dans le domaine social, Astrasbourg, 25-27 Novembre.

Council of Europe. (1986). *Violence in the family.* Recommendation No R (85) 4. Strasbourg.

Council of Europe. (1990). Committee of Ministers. Recommendation No R (90) 2.

Kanellopoulos, K. N. (1984). *The aged in Greece: A statistical analysis of their socioeconomic characteristics.* Centre of Planning and Economic Research (KEPE), Athens, Greece.

Loizos-Malikiossi, M. (1986). *The impact of social cohesion and time available for assistance to the elderly.* European Foundation for the Improvement of Living and Working Conditions, Dublin, Ireland.

National Statistical Service of Greece. (1961-1981). *Population census.* Athens, Greece.

Pitsiou, E. (1986). *Life styles of older Athenians.* National Centre of Social Research, Athens, Greece.

Pitsiou, E. (1986). *Social and psychological adaptation to aging among older Athenians.* National Centre of Social Research, Athens, Greece.

Police Journal. (Greek) Volumes, June 1987-December 1988.

Schneider, H. J. (1987). *Criminology.* Berlin/New York: de Gruyter Lehrbuch.

Spinellis, C. D. (1985). *Criminology.* Athens, Greece: Sakkoula.

Spinellis, C. D. (1990). Family violence: Current analysis of the problem. In *The Greek victimology,* Volume #1. Violence in the Family. Athens, Greece.

Spinellis, C. D. & Pitsiou-Darrough, E. (1991a). *Elderly victims of abuse and neglect,* EKLOGH, Athens, Greece.

Spinellis, C. D. & Pitsiou-Darrough, E. (1991b). Elder abuse in Greece: A descriptive study. In: G. Kaizer, H. Kurry & H.-J. Albrecht (Eds.), *Victims and criminal justice* (pp. 311-338). Freiburg: Eigenverlag Max-Planck-Institute.

United Nations, Seventh U.N. Congress on the Prevention of Crime and the Treatment of Offenders.

Chapter 5

Elder Abuse in Hong Kong:
A New Family Problem for the Old East?

Alex Yui-huen Kwan, PhD

INTRODUCTION

In 1982, the World Assembly on Aging (held by the United Nations in Vienna) called for "Concern on Aging." The elderly population is the fastest growing sector of the world's population and by the year 2000 there will be 590 million people over age 60 (United Nations, 1984). Between 1950 and 2025, the world population will grow by a factor of more than three; the elderly population by a factor of six; and the old-old by a factor of ten. These trends have major policy implications. Every day that passes sees about 30,000 people crossing the threshold of 60 (Anstee, 1989). By the year 2025, there are projected to be more than a billion people above 60 years of age in the world. Over 70 percent of them are likely to be living in developing regions (Anstee, 1989).

The aging population in modern industrial society has to face

Alex Yui-huen Kwan is Principal Lecturer, Department of Applied Social Studies, City Polytechnic of Hong Kong, 83 Tat Chee Avenue, Kowloon, Hong Kong.

An earlier version of this paper was presented at the Adult Protective Services Conference in San Antonio, Texas, November 5-8, 1991.

[Haworth co-indexing entry note]: "Elder Abuse in Hong Kong: A New Family Problem for the Old East?" Kwan, Alex Yui-huen. Co-published simultaneously in the *Journal of Elder Abuse & Neglect* (The Haworth Press, Inc.) Vol. 6, No. 3/4, 1995, pp. 65-80; and: *Elder Abuse: International and Cross-Cultural Perspectives* (ed: Jordan I. Kosberg, and Juanita L. Garcia) The Haworth Press, Inc., 1995, pp. 65-80. Multiple copies of this article/chapter may be purchased from The Haworth Document Delivery Center [1-800-3-HAWORTH; 9:00 a.m. - 5:00 p.m. (EST)].

many difficulties after retirement. These difficulties are related to rapid demographic and socioeconomic changes. Chan (1988) observed that these changes can alter traditional values, family life-cycle and structure, kinship relations, the role and status of the aged, and support networks, all of which may adversely affect the well-being of the aged population. Among all the difficulties the elderly are facing, one that is attracting worldwide attention is the problem of elder abuse.

Research on family violence in the 1970s called attention to elder abuse in Great Britain and in the United States (Giordano & Giordano, 1984). Since then the problem of elder abuse has been recognized worldwide. Recently, there have been research reports of elder abuse in Canada (Brillon, 1987; McDonald et al., 1991); Denmark and Sweden (Tornstam, 1989); Japan (Kaneko & Yamada, 1990); Israel (Wolf & Bergman, 1989); Norway (Hydle, 1989); Ghana (Brown, 1987); Germany, Belgium, Portugal, Italy, France and Finland (Hydle, 1988); Europe (Council of Europe, 1984); and Western Europe (Hydle, 1989a). This paper will specifically focus on elder abuse in Hong Kong, a predominantly Chinese society in the Far East.

Hong Kong in Cultural Context

Clearly, the meaning of aging and the importance of the behavior of others toward the elderly within a society cannot be accurately assessed in isolation. One must pay close attention to the ethos of the people and the cultural value system within which these phenomena are embedded. One of the value systems that has obvious and profound implications for the condition and status of the elderly in a society is the value imperative for "filial piety."

Traditional Chinese culture, in contrast to beliefs and attitudes in the West, emphasized that elderly people should be revered (Koo, 1984), respected, and provided comfort and leisure in old age. Thus, people looked forward to being old. The period of old age for the Chinese began roughly around the age of 55. Unless they had been unfortunate enough not to have had children, the aging Chinese couple had little to worry about in their declining years. Old age implied that one had greater experience, wisdom, status, and power in the family system. Thus, those in "later maturity" occupied a secure status, received formal deference, and were objects of great respect (Queen et al., 1985).

The two major philosophical traditions, Confucianism and Taoism, also emphasized reverence for longevity. As observed by Baker (1979), Confucius taught that there were Five Human Relationship Pairs: ruler and minister, father and son, elder brother and younger brother, husband and wife, and elder and younger person. The relationships are arranged in order of priority. When these relationships are rightly constituted, the health of the entire society is maintained. Confucianism considered filial piety to be the root of all virtue. The young were taught through Confucian doctrines that they were obligated to respect, care for, and obey their elders (Cowgill, 1986). Those who did not care for their parents were heavily criticized or even ostracized from society (Dawson, 1915). The Taoist tradition tried to find means of prolonging life by developing various medicines and advocating changes in lifestyle that were believed to increase longevity (Koo, 1984). The traditional governmental and judicial systems also reinforced the obligation of filial piety. Thus, it can be said that one's duty to respect and care for elders, especially if they were related kinsmen, was institutionalized in Chinese society through Confucianism, Taoism and public policy.

Aging in Hong Kong

The present population of Hong Kong is estimated to be approximately 5.9 million people (Census and Statistics Department, 1986). As Table 1 reflects, the number of people age 60 and over was estimated to be 640,300 (11.6%) in mid-1986 and is expected to rise to 909,500 (14.1%) in mid-2001 (Chow, 1980). This trend is mainly brought about by (1) a low birth rate, (2) lower mortality rates in childhood and young adulthood, and (3) increasingly longer life expectancy, which was estimated to be 74.7 for male and 80.3 for females in 1989, and is anticipated to rise to 76.5 for males and 82.2 for females by the year 1999 (Working Party on Social Welfare Policies and Services, 1990). Increasing numbers of elderly persons will result in a corresponding increase in the demand for greater number, variety, and duration of services for the elderly.

In order to better understand why elder abuse exists in a traditional Chinese culture, it is necessary to identify the changes which

TABLE 1. The Older Population of Hong Kong.

Year	Total Population	60+	%	65+	%
1976	4,518,000	399,900	8.9	244,500	5.4
1981	5,163,100	530,900	10.3	343,900	6.7
1986	5,524,300	640,300	11.6	424,300	7.7
1991	5,921,600	759,100	12.8	517,900	8.7
1996	6,229,200	851,100	13.7	608,900	9.8
2001	6,446,000	909,500	14.1	674,100	10.5

are affecting the structure and values of the Colony (Lau, 1984). Starak (1988) indicated that in Hong Kong there is a state of tension between the traditional family structures (a source of stability) and the new family customs threatening the old social fabric. The present structure of families in Hong Kong is a transitional one, continuously adjusting itself to the forces of social change. As suggested by Yeung (1989), the primary social support system for many elderly persons has been weakened in recent years. The small size of public housing units has directly or indirectly discouraged young couples from living with their aging parents. As young couples with children move to new towns outside urban Hong Kong, many elderly people are left behind in the deteriorating residential areas in the town centers.

The elderly are no longer respected by most people in Hong Kong (Chow, 1987). There is ample evidence that the restructuring of the basic support networks of elderly is occurring in Hong Kong (Chan and Yeung, 1991). Industrialization and urbanization have increased rapidly over the past 30 years. Although responsible for Hong Kong's prosperity, these processes also have their negative side-effects such as the rapid increase of suicide among older persons (Kwan, 1988).

Prolonged life expectancy and the decline in birth rates have had an impact on families. The empty nest and retirement period in the family life-cycle is expanding, calling for more and better services for elderly people living in the community. In the past five years, up to 205,000 Hong Kong residents have migrated to other countries leaving behind approximately 30,000 older persons, many of whom have no other informal support systems and unfilled social service needs (Wu, 1991). From a recent study, Leung (1991) reported that older persons currently experience more interpersonal problems within their family due to social changes. Among the 662 clients of multi-service centers for the elderly, 31% experienced interpersonal difficulties, and 35.8% experienced housing problems. The increasing hardships being encountered by the elderly are further confirmed by a study of the coping behavior of caregivers in Hong Kong (Kwan, 1991a). The study found that most caregivers (88%) were forced to care for an elderly person because no other alternatives were available. And, in general, the caregivers did not receive enough respite support in their caring for the elderly from either family members or formal resources.

With the increased realization that traditional family support networks in Hong Kong were inadequate (Chi and Lee, 1989; Kwan, 1989) and with the government's guiding principle of "care in the community and by the community" as expressed in the 1979 White Paper (Social Welfare Department, 1979), a wide range of community support services is provided to help families look after their elderly members and to enable old people to live in the community for as long as possible. At the end of 1990, there were 60 home help teams, 124 social centers, 17 multi-service centers and nine day care centers. Thirty-seven respite care beds for the elderly were also available in homes for the elderly. In addition, there were 6,828 beds in hostels/homes for the elderly and 3,163 beds in care-and-attention homes. Finally 3,485 elderly people, capable of living independently, were provided housing in sheltered housing flats (Government Information Services, 1991).

With the sheer number of persons aged 60 and above (759,100) in the Hong Kong community, the social umbrella provided for the elderly has many holes in its fabric (Kwan, 1991). For example, the waiting time for priority allocation of public housing is six to seven years (Hong Kong Council on Social Services, 1987). In 1988, there were more than 7,000 elderly persons waiting for admission into infirmary and care-and-attention placements (Chow, 1988). Furthermore, many of the residents of the more than 300 private nursing homes have been found to be dissatisfied with the provision of psychosocial care (Kwan, 1988a). Even the government has acknowledged that there are significant shortfalls in the current provision of social welfare services for the elderly (Social Welfare Department, 1991). Since a supportive formal and informal care system is not yet established in Hong Kong, a large proportion of elderly in Hong Kong are at-risk of being abused.

ELDER ABUSE RESEARCH

In Hong Kong, with its predominantly Chinese inhabitants, where filial piety has been treated as a sacred norm, the existence of "elder abuse" may be surprising to many. Yet, there is an increasing number of elderly abandoned at local hospitals. One reporter estimated that roughly 90-100 older persons are abandoned each month in Hong Kong hospitals (Chan, 1985). The following is an incident reported in the *South China Morning Post* of June 17, 1976, which received wide coverage by local newspaper and television news programs:

> A 65-year-old woman who spent four days on the Macau hydrofoil wharf waiting for her son to return with her travel documents finally got back to Hong Kong yesterday with the help of friends. Madam Lee was taken to Macau two weeks ago by her son and daughter-in-law for medical treatment. Once there, her son (38 years of age) put her in a boarding house and gave her HK$200 (US$25). The couple then took her identity card and travel documents and told her to wait three to four days for their return. She stayed at the boarding house for ten days until her money ran out and then took up her vigil at the hydrofoil wharf.

This incident is only one of many accounts reported recently. However, the lack of an acceptable definition of intrafamilial abuse continues to be a significant impediment to understanding extent, patterns, and causes (Giordano & Giordano, 1984). Hudson and Johnson (1987) reviewed 31 empirical studies on elder abuse and found that physical and psychological abuse are uniformly included in definitions of elder abuse. However, distinctions between active and passive neglect and separate classifications of financial, material, or economic abuse, medical abuse, exploitation, violation of rights, self-neglect, and self-abuse vary from study to study (Connidis, 1989; Hornick, McDonald, Robertson, & Wallace, 1988; McDonald et al., 1991; Schlesinger & Schlesinger, 1988). In a recent meeting of the National Aging Resource Center on Elder Abuse, researchers still disagreed over such basic issues as how abuse should be defined and what types of maltreatment should be considered (Stein, 1991). Because there is variability in the definitions employed in research on elder abuse, comparing the results of different studies is difficult, if not impossible.

Though discussions around the elder abuse issue have witnessed a drastic increase in recent years, there have been only two empirical studies (Chan, 1985; Leung, 1989) on elder abuse conducted in Hong Kong. A brief summary of their findings follows.

Study 1: A Study on Elder Abuse at Home in Hong Kong

In the first study, Chan (1985) began by gathering 153 abuse indicators from social work practitioners through a preliminary opinion survey. Next, 220 professional key informants identified 45 separate items from the pool, compressed them into 24 indicators of elder abuse, and grouped them into four categories: physical abuse, abuse in daily living, financial abuse and psychological abuse. By using the 24 definitive indicators, a total of 93 cases of elder abuse, identified by social and health service agency staff, were studied in detail. A case-by-case analysis determined the total number of clients who manifested the characteristics similar to those developed in the indicators.

Fifteen abuse indicators were further selected and incorporated into five vignettes which were used in a territory-wide opinion survey. The survey examined the views of people who had elderly living with them to see how many would use "abuse" as a way to resolve daily problems with their elderly. A total of 637 representatives from households with older persons were interviewed. From the case study, several variables were found to be associated with being a victim of elder abuse: being 70 years of age and older, a female, widowed, poorly educated, financially dependent upon a family caregiver, less able to care for oneself, in poorer health, a member of a larger household, and having little social involvement and poor family relationships (Chan, 1985). In terms of projection, the survey estimated that 136,000 old persons in Hong Kong (22.6% of the total elderly population) would be at-risk of being abused (Chan, 1985).

Study 2: A Study on Elder Abuse in Tuen Mun Public Housing Estates

Leung (1989) interviewed a total of 150 caregivers in Tuen Mun areas and observed that most of the care-receivers were widowed, without formal education, experiencing poor health, and heavily dependent upon family caregivers. The findings also suggested that caregivers were more likely to engage in psychological abuse rather than physical abuse. As to the possible correlates of elder abuse, the study found that abuse was significantly and positively related to the level of stress, informal support, and physical assistance received by the caregivers (Leung, 1989).

DISCUSSION

As suggested by Kosberg and Kwan (1989), differences in definitions of elder abuse in Hong Kong and in the United States are overshadowed by the similarities. The studies reviewed in this paper support the fact that elders who are the most vulnerable are more likely to be abused, including the oldest, the most impaired, the most dependent, and most isolated.

Despite the recent attention devoted to elder abuse and neglect as social problems, the causes of these phenomena are largely unknown. Empirical evidence about predictors of elder abuse is scarce and there is a corresponding lack of empirically generated and tested theoretical propositions on the causes of abuse and neglect of the elderly (McDonald et al., 1991). Existing studies do, however, offer a place to begin and can help in efforts to consider general theories of causation. Quinn and Tomita (1986) grouped the causes of abuse into five categories: physical and mental impairment of an older adult, the effect of stress on the caregiver, the influence of families which have learned to solve problems by being violent with one another, intraindividual problems of the abuser, and societal attitudes (as contributors to elder abuse and neglect). Anetzberger (1987) also suggested five dominant explanations for elder abuse: four relate to the perpetrator (abuse socialization, pathology, stress and social isolation) and one to the victim (vulnerability).

Recently, McDonald et al. (1991) pointed out that much of the literature does not make an important distinction between theoretical explanations and causal factors related to elder abuse and neglect. They had identified three theories (the situational model, social exchange theory, and the symbolic interaction approach) that can be used to explain elder abuse and neglect. Furthermore, each of these three theoretical explanations incorporated a variety of causal factors that are hypothesized to be associated with elder abuse and neglect. Such factors included transgenerational family violence, dependencies, personality traits of the abuser, filial crisis, internal and external stressors, social isolation, societal attitudes towards the elderly, and institutional factors.

Policy and Program Recommendations

As the older population continues to age, the proportion living in the community who need personal care will increase. This is true for Hong Kong and most (if not all) of the countries in the world. The intensity and frequency of needed care will increase as well, along with the risk of being abused. Since the increasing problem of elder abuse has been acknowledged in Hong Kong, a number of intervention programs and services have been recommended (Chan, 1985; Leung, 1988, 1988a, 1989). From the West, examples for needed programs and services to be adopted in Hong Kong have been provided by Quinn and Tomita (1986), Anetzberger (1987), Roff and Atherton (1989), and McDonald et al. (1991) among others.

Current social welfare policy in Hong Kong emphasizes the importance of family (Social Welfare Department, 1991), especially adult sons and daughters, in assuming greater responsibility for the care of elderly persons. The rationale for this is both philosophically and fiscally based. Yet, not all adult offspring have the capacity to assume such responsibility. A major step in working with, as well as preventing, cases of abuse would be to acknowledge the family's contribution to the care of the elderly person and to provide services that support and enhance the caregiving role. Families who agree to look after old people should receive more help. Weekday or weekend day centers, and temporary accommodation schemes for holiday periods, should be developed in order to make the caregiving responsibility more acceptable and preserve the equilibrium of the family as well as that of the old person. Other needed services include home nursing care, homemakers, home health aides, home-delivered meals, home repair, home visitation programs, telephone reassurance, outreach services, adult day care, overnight respite care, and transportation. Family life education and counseling services to support the family's efforts and to focus upon emotional strains associated with caregiving also should be available.

Not only does social welfare policy need to support families that can effectively assume the caregiving role, it also needs to provide viable caregiving alternatives when families decline to perform this role. Recall, the exodus from Hong Kong by younger persons is leaving an increasing number of elderly persons who have no family to provide care for them. Minimally, these alternatives should include sound, low cost and well-publicized residential facilities ranging from adult family care and assisted living through nursing home care. A variety of support services are required to prevent elder abuse by filial caregivers. Supplements for incompetent families should include respite care and homemaker-home health aide services. Adequate leaves from work should be provided to employees, so as to enable them to take care of sick relatives or to receive relief from medical care. The promotion of neighborhood schemes should be encouraged, so that people can provide day-to-day practical help for the old. Housing subsidies should be given to families taking an elderly person into their household or who provide a separate neighboring flat.

Social service agencies can assist prospective caregivers to assess the probability of abuse and support them through counseling regarding caregiving decisions. For service providers, ways must be found to detect potentially abusive situations and, thereby, to prevent the occurrence of abuse. Prospective caregivers, having a large number of identified abuse-prone characteristics, may wish to seek alternatives to assuming a caregiving role for the elder parent. Hospitals and other health facilities need to establish elder abuse detection protocols and procedures. Mental health and mental retardation service systems need to become more involved in preventing and treating elder abuse. Since a major factor explaining physical abuse seems to be pathology on the part of the perpetrator, the various service systems most concerned with pathology must assume roles in helping impaired offspring make appropriate decisions for the care of an elderly parent. These systems must also provide treatment to alleviate emotional damage caused by inappropriate caregiving.

Finally, government service planners and community advocates for the aged in Hong Kong need to advance a national policy on the elder abuse issue. The policy should recognize that the family and government in Hong Kong are partners in the provision of care to the elder at risk of abuse. The government should assume a leadership and coordinating role over the public and the voluntary sectors in working out guidelines for handling elder abuse. The government should also institute a comprehensive protective service system for vulnerable elderly, as found in many states in the U.S., with the authority to intervene in cases of abuse or maltreatment.

CONCLUSION

The diversity of formal responses to the needs of older people, and the highly variable level of in-cash and in-kind benefits offered to them by the Hong Kong government, leave many needs of the elderly unsatisfied. These discrepancies between needs and resources will become more important as demographic trends in the coming decades considerably increase the number of old people. Coordination of social welfare policies, therefore, is essential to avoid the sacrifice of old people who are costly, both in terms of direct social security payments and the services provided to enhance autonomy on the altar of economic competition.

It would, indeed, seem essential for the Hong Kong government to continue campaigning to improve the living standards of the old, to help to keep the elderly in their natural, family environment, to adapt their collective care facilities to meet the needs of the population and to coordinate and plan health and social welfare work for their benefit. If well conceived and implemented, such a social welfare policy may obviate some of the negative effects of aging, prevent many older individuals from becoming abused, and ensure that their later years are happy at less cost to the community.

Though, on paper, the Hong Kong government suggests that "innovation, flexibility and integration in the design and delivery of programs and services must be accorded greater emphasis to ensure that limited resources are utilized to the optimum and that access by clients to a comprehensive range of services is improved" (Social Welfare Department, 1991), the following questions concerning the nature of governmental programs on aging still require answers:

1. What type of agency is needed at the community level to serve as a focal point for broad action in elder abuse? What should its functions be?
2. What is the most desirable method of integrating or inter-relating the activities of strengthening the family system in Hong Kong?
3. How can we increase the ability of various welfare agencies to muster the political power needed to enact legislation in elder abuse?

In the West, despite the voluminous literature devoted to the topic, knowledge about elder abuse is still inconclusive. In Hong Kong, even less is known about the incidence and prevalence of elder abuse and neglect. Still less is known about why it occurs, under what circumstances, and how to prevent such incidents or alleviate their effects. Because of the imprecision in definitions of elder abuse and neglect and the differences between the two concepts, the extent of these problems is not known in Hong Kong. Nevertheless, an inability to identify the social parameters of elder abuse and neglect in Hong Kong should not prevent the Hong Kong government from developing policies.

In conclusion, elder abuse and neglect are not the major concern or responsibility of one profession, one individual, or one nation. Rather, all of those involved must address the issues, questions, and concerns raised everywhere in the world. More and more developing and under-developed countries in the world are likely to discover the problems of elder abuse. People from countries that have studied the dynamics of elder abuse should share their findings with others, to both increase understanding and encourage preventive and interventive efforts for the welfare of the older population. If our dream in 1990s is to build a world in which our young can develop and grow, perhaps, the challenge for the 2000s is to build a world in which the old may live and die in dignity.

REFERENCES

Anetzberger, G.J. (1987). *The etiology of elder abuse by adult offspring.* Springfield, Illinois: Charles C Thomas.
Anstee, M.J. (1989). Impact of the aging world. *Hong Kong Journal of Gerontology, 3* (1), 3-5.

Baker, H.D.R. (1979). *Chinese family and kinship.* New York: Columbia University Press.

Brillon, I. (1987). *Victimization and fear of crime among the elderly.* Vancouver, British Columbia: Butterworths.

Brown, C.K. (1987). *Social structure and aging: A comparative study of the status of the aging in the United States and Ghana.* Report submitted to the Council for International Exchange of Scholars. Atlanta, GA: Atlanta University.

Census and Statistics Department. (1986). *Hong Kong 1986 by-census: Summary results.* Hong Kong: Government Printer.

Chan H.T. (1985). *Report of elderly abuse at home in Hong Kong.* Hong Kong: Hong Kong Council of Social Services.

Chan Y.K. (1988). Modern society and aged population. *Hong Kong Journal of Gerontology, 2* (1), 37-39.

Chan, W.T. and Yeung, W.T. (1991). The social situations of elderly in Hong Kong. *Social Welfare Quarterly, 116,* 1-5.

Chi, I. & Lee, J.J. (1989). *Client health survey of the elderly in Hong Kong.* Hong Kong: Department of Social Work and Social Administration, University of Hong Kong.

Chow, W.S. (1980). Changing characteristics of the elderly population in Hong Kong. In Hong Kong Society for the Aged, proceeding on the seminar on the elderly. Hong Kong: Authentic Printing Company.

Chow, W.S. (1987). Factors influencing the support of the elderly by their family. *Hong Kong Journal of Gerontology, 1* (1), 4-9.

Chow, W.S. (1988). *Caregiving for the elderly awaiting admission into care and attention homes.* Hong Kong: Department of Social Work and Social Administration, University of Hong Kong.

Connidis, I.A. (1989). *Family ties and aging.* Toronto: Butterworths.

Council of Europe. (1984). *The social protection of the very old.* Strasburg, France: Council of Europe.

Cowgill, D.O. (1986). *Aging around the world.* California: Wadsworth.

Dawson, M.M. (1915). *The ethics of Confucius.* New York: Putnam.

Douglass, R.L. (1983). Domestic needs and abuse of the elderly: Implications for research and service. *Family Relations, 32,* 395-402.

Giordano, N.H. & Giordano, J.A. (1984). Elder abuse: A review of the literature. *Social Work, 29* (2), 232-236.

Government Information Services. (1991). *Hong Kong 1991.* Hong Kong: Government Printer.

Hong Kong Council of Social Services. (1987). *A report on the housing needs of older persons in Hong Kong.* Hong Kong: Hong Kong Council of Social Services.

Hornick, J., McDonald, L., Robertson, G. & Wallace, J.E. (1988). *A review of the social and legal issues concerning elder abuse.* Calgary, Alberta: Canadian Research Institute for Law and the Family.

Hudson, M.F. & Johnson T.F. (1987). Elder neglect and abuse: A review of the literature. M. C. Eisdorfer (ed.) *Annual review of gerontology.* New York: Springer.

Hydle, I. (1988). *Violence against the elderly in Western Europe–Measures in the health and social fields.* Oslo, Norway: Department of Geriatrics, Ulleval Hospital and University of Oslo.

Hydle, I. (1989). *Elder abuse and neglect in the family–A proposal for a European interdisciplinary project.* Oslo, Norway: Department of Geriatrics, Ulleval Hospital.

Hydle, I. (1989a). Violence against the elderly in Western Europe–Treatment and preventive measures in the health and social service fields. *Journal of Elder Abuse & Neglect, 1,* (3), 75-87.

Kaneko, Y. & Yamada, Y. (1990). Wives and mothers-in-law: Potential for family conflict in post-war Japan. *Journal of Elder Abuse & Neglect, 2* (1/2), 87-98.

Koo, L.C. (1984). Traditional Chinese concepts towards the elderly. In Mental Health Association of Hong Kong, *Mental health and old age* (pp. 61-64). Hong Kong: Mental Health Association of Hong Kong.

Kosberg, J.I. & Kwan, Y.H. (1989). *Elder abuse in Hong Kong and the United States: A comparative analysis with international implications.* Paper presented at the Symposium on Cross-cultural Perspectives on Elder Abuse, International Congress of Gerontology, Acapulco, Mexico, June 1989.

Kwan. Y.H. (1988). Suicide among the elderly: Hong Kong. *The Journal of Applied Gerontology, 7* (2), 248-259.

Kwan, Y.H. (1988a). *A study of the life-style of the residents of private homes for the elderly in Hong Kong.* Hong Kong: Writers' and Publishers' Cooperative.

Kwan, Y.H. (Ed.) (1989). *Hong Kong Society.* Hong Kong: Writers' and Publishers' Cooperative.

Kwan, Y.H. (1991). The social changes of family and the development of welfare services for elderly in Hong Kong. In K. Kiu (Ed.), *Chinese family and its changes* (pp. 357-369). Hong Kong: Chinese University of Hong Kong Press.

Kwan, Y.H. (1991a). *A study of the coping behavior of caregivers in Hong Kong.* Hong Kong: Writers' and Publishers' Cooperative.

Lau, W.L. (1984). Social changes and elderly. In Mental Health Association of Hong Kong, *Mental health and old age* (pp. 64-72). Hong Kong: Mental Health Association of Hong Kong.

Leung, W.H. (1988). Social services for abused elderly. In Hong Kong Society for the Aged, *Proceeding of seminar on services for the elderly* (pp. 88-96). Hong Kong: Hong Kong Society for the Aged.

Leung, W.H. (1988a). Formation of a multidisciplinary team to deal with elderly abuse cases–Reality and fantasy? *Hong Kong Journal of Gerontology, 2* (1), 43-46.

Leung, W.H. (1989). Elderly abuse in Tuen Mun public housing estates. *Hong Kong Journal of Gerontology, 3,* (1), 6-9.

Leung, W.H. (1991). The family relationship of older persons. *Social Welfare Quarterly, 116,* 11-15.

McDonald, P.L., Hornick, J.P., Robertson, G.B. & Wallace, J.E. (1991). *Elder abuse and neglect in Canada*. Toronto: Butterworths.

Queen, S.A., Haberstein, R.W. and Quadagno, J.S. (1985). *The family in various cultures* (5th ed.). New York: Harper & Row.

Quinn, M.J. & Tomita, S.K. (1986). *Elder abuse and neglect: Causes, diagnosis, and intervention strategies*. New York: Springer.

Roff, L.L. & Atherton, C.R. (1989). *Promoting successful aging*. Chicago: Nelson-Hall.

Schlesinger, B. & Schlesinger, R. (1988). *Abuse of the elderly: Issues and annotated bibliography*. Toronto: University of Toronto Press.

Social Welfare Department. (1979). *Social welfare into the 1980s*. Hong Kong: Government Printer.

Social Welfare Department. (1991). *White paper on social welfare into the 1990s and beyond*. Hong Kong: Government Printer.

Starak, Y. (1988). Hong Kong: A model of 'social happiness' for the new China. *International Social Work, 31*, (3), 211-217.

Stein, K.F. (1991). A national agenda for elder abuse and neglect research: Issues and recommendations. *Journal of Elder Abuse & Neglect, 3*, (3), 91-108.

The Working Party on Social Welfare Policies and Services. (1990). *Draft white paper on social welfare into the 1990s and beyond*. Hong Kong: Government Printer.

Tornstam, L. (1989). Abuse of the elderly in Denmark and Sweden: Results from a population study. *Journal of Elder Abuse & Neglect, 1* (1), 35-44.

United Nations. (1984). *Selected documents from the world assembly on aging*. New York: International Center of Social Gerontology.

Wolf, R.S. & Bergman, S. (Eds.) (1989). *Stress, conflict and abuse of the elderly*. Jerusalem, Israel: Institute of Gerontology and Adult Human Development.

Wu, S.S. (1991). The problems of older persons caused by migration. *Social Welfare Quarterly, 116*, 22-26.

Yeung, W.T. (1989). The changing family system in Hong Kong. In Y.H. Kwan (Ed.), *Hong Kong Society* (pp. 185-212). Hong Kong: Writers' and Publishers' Cooperative.

Chapter 6

Elder Abuse in a Forming Society: Israel

Ariela Lowenstein, PhD

INTRODUCTION

In the United States and in some European countries, the decade of the 1980s was devoted to elder abuse (Kosberg, 1988). In Israel, during that decade, an examination of the issues of violence in the family, mainly child abuse and spouse abuse, was begun. Professional and public attention to elder abuse as a social phenomenon and a social problem is just emerging. The enactment of a special piece of legislation, The 1989 Law of Protection of the Helpless, gave the impetus to address the topic of elder abuse. It reflects the awareness by policymakers and legislators of the vulnerability of certain segments of the aged. It is a natural outcome of dealing with other forms of family violence that are no longer taboo, even in a society that strongly values the family and emphasizes family care.

As the study of the phenomenon of elder abuse is only in its beginning stages, very little data are available. This chapter will

Ariela Lowenstein is Director, Center for Research and Study of Aging, School of Social Work, Haifa University, Haifa.

The author wishes to express her appreciation to her dear colleague, Professor Simon Bergman, for his guidance, review, and useful remarks.

[Haworth co-indexing entry note]: "Elder Abuse in a Forming Society: Israel." Lowenstein, Ariela. Co-published simultaneously in the *Journal of Elder Abuse & Neglect* (The Haworth Press, Inc.) Vol. 6, No. 3/4, 1995, pp. 81-100; and: *Elder Abuse: International and Cross-Cultural Perspectives* (ed: Jordan I. Kosberg, and Juanita L. Garcia) The Haworth Press, Inc., 1995, pp. 81-100. Multiple copies of this article/chapter may be purchased from The Haworth Document Delivery Center [1-800-3-HAWORTH; 9:00 a.m. - 5:00 p.m. (EST)].

thus outline the demography of the Israeli scene and the role of the family in Israeli society and Jewish tradition. The outcome of the aging of the population, which increases the burden of care on informal and formal systems, will be analyzed regarding possible instances and causes of elder abuse. The main social control mechanisms will be presented and the central dilemmas discussed.

DEMOGRAPHIC TRENDS AND FAMILY CARE OF THE ELDERLY

Israel is a country where "immigration is a central phenomenon of its existence. Without it Israel could never have come into being, nor can it sustain itself and its continuation. In it lies the nation's historical raison d'etre as the haven for those in need and as the spiritual, cultural, and historical center it can offer to Jews in other countries" (Bergman, 1980, p. 208). The recent large waves of immigrants from the former Soviet Union and from Ethiopia reflect this outlook.

One of the unusual aspects of the waves of immigration into Israel is the fact that some 8 percent of the immigrants were at least 60 years of age at the time of their arrival. Thus, even today, what characterizes the Jewish elderly in Israel is that they are predominantly foreign born: 71 percent from Europe and America, 25 percent from Asia and Africa, and only 4 percent were born in Israel. About 28 percent arrived before 1948 and the remaining 68 percent were post-1948 immigrants from every possible corner of the world (Bergman & Lowenstein, 1988).

During the last decade, the aging of the Israeli population has become a focus of public attention. Not only has the percentage of the Jewish population aged 65 and older grown from slightly more than 5 percent (numbering 100,000) in 1960 to 10 percent in the 1990s (numbering close to 450,000), but a significant change has also occurred in the composition of the aged: they are growing older. The share of those aged 75 and older within the 65-plus population reached 40 percent in 1990, and the over-85 group will grow by almost 100 percent during the 1990s, and will continue to grow rapidly until the end of the century. The overall dependency ratio in Israel is, thus, higher than the average found in developed countries: 71 as compared with 55 dependents to 100 non-dependents in developed countries (Sabatello, 1989; CBS, 1989; Morginstin, 1990; Be'er & Factor, 1990; Barnea & Habib, 1992). The majority of the aged reside in the three largest cities: Tel-Aviv, Jerusalem, and Haifa. By gender, there is a slightly larger number of females, especially pronounced in the 80 and older group of which females constitute 55 percent.

Israel is distinguished from European countries by its much lower proportion of older people living alone and a higher proportion of couples. In all countries except Israel, single females are the most prevalent individuals among the 75 and older group. They constitute 50 percent of all families in Sweden, Norway, and West Germany and 45 percent in the United States, Canada, and the United Kingdom. In Israel, only 23 percent of all households in the 75 plus group are single females, while the percentage of couples without children is 47 percent. This difference between Israel and other countries apparently stems from its relatively low rate of divorces and separations. Family size is, in large measure, attributed to household composition. In Israel, elderly families are larger than in other countries (Achdut & Tamir, 1986; Shmueli, 1989; Morginstin, 1990).

In 1989, it was estimated that close to 26 percent of the elderly lived with their children. Studies revealed that country of origin, sex, and family status were the major sociodemographic characteristics associated with living arrangements of the elderly (Shmueli, 1989). For example, elderly from Western origin live mostly with a daughter, those from Eastern origin (Asia-Africa) live mostly with a son (Morginstin & Cohen, 1980; Shmueli, 1989). Data also show that 84 percent of the elderly with children see them at least once a week (Scuval, 1982; Noam, 1989).

In Israel, only about 5 percent of the aged are in residential settings. This is mainly due to the strong sense of filial responsibility and the tradition of several cultural and ethnic-religious groups within the general population, such as the Oriental Jews and the Arabs (both Muslim and Christian), against institutionalizing elderly parents (Guttmann & Lowenstein, forthcoming). Thus, as data from various surveys document, the major source of care of those dependent elderly living in the community is the family (Zilberstein, 1981; Shuval, 1982; Noam, 1989).

ELDER ABUSE IN ISRAEL

A society that has crystallized itself around immigration faces special problems in family care. Cultural, social, and population heterogeneity of Israel increases the vulnerability of certain sub-segments of the elderly for exposure to situational and environmental contexts that might facilitate the possibility of risk to abuse.

Abuse of the elderly had been termed "one of modern times best kept secrets" (South Africa Council on Aging, 1992); "an unnecessary and preventable problem" (Tomlin, 1992); "a hidden problem" and "a national disgrace" (U.S. Congress, 1981, 1985). However, it is hard to find any national prevalence studies, even in the United States where the problem was "discovered" by the research community during the decade of the 1980s. Most studies report between 4 to 10 percent of the elderly being abused, depending on the definitions of abuse and the methodologies used (Lau & Kosberg, 1979; Block & Sinnott, 1979; Rathbone-McCuan, 1980; Sengstock & Liang, 1982; Wolf et al., 1982; Hickey & Douglass, 1983; Giordano & Giordano, 1984; Poertner, 1986; Pillemer & Wolf, 1986; Pillemer & Finkelhor, 1988; Wolf, 1992). According to these estimates, the number of abused elders in Israel could range from 20,000 to 50,000 (between 4 percent to 10 percent of the elderly). However, due to the specific context of the Israeli society, one cannot easily compare it with statistics obtained from other countries.

One may "typologize" the settings in which elder abuse could occur into three broad categories: first, *the family setting*, especially those where direct care provision is needed; second, *the network of community services* to older people–services provided in the homes and those frequently used by elderly people (such as day care centers, clubs, etc.); and third, the variety of *residential settings*, from sheltered housing through old age homes and nursing homes.

This discussion will focus on the potential of exposure to abuse by direct caregivers in the community, mainly family members. The problems of elder abuse in the network of community services and in residential settings will be presented more briefly. The reasons for such an emphasis are twofold: first, only a small minority of elderly persons live in institutional settings and second, the abundance of literature is on elder abuse by family caregivers.

Types of 'At-Risk' Abuse Within the "Family Setting"

It is well-documented in the literature that family relationships greatly influence the well-being of the elderly and provide support that may prevent or postpone the need for formal services and institutionalization. From the literature it is also evident, however, that aged persons who live with others are at higher risk for abuse compared to those living alone (O'Malley, 1979; Wolf, 1986). Also, dependent elderly in poor health are found to be three to four more times likely to be abused than the well, independent elderly (Lau & Kosberg, 1979; Steinmetz, 1983; Wolf, 1986; Quinn & Tomita, 1986; Anetzberger, 1987). Thus, researchers on family and elder abuse have been especially interested in elderly living together with their children who are their direct caregivers.

One of the most difficult consequences of caregivers' ineffective coping is found to be abuse of the care receiver. Most instances of abuse are not intentional but result from the accumulation of stress and limited resources for providing care. In many cases, caregivers do not recognize their abusiveness; those who acknowledge it often are at a loss to know how to stop their harmful behavior (Horowitz & Shindelman, 1983; Steinmetz, 1988; Young & Kahana, 1989).

Might the situation be similar in Israel? Does this picture, pointing to the relationship between increased levels of dependency, family stress and abuse, also apply to Israeli family caregivers? In other words, who are the persons most at-risk of abuse within the family setting in Israel?

In Israel, as was mentioned, a relatively large percentage (26%) of the elderly live with their children, especially those 75 years of age and older. It is documented that the fastest-growing segment of the older population is aged 75 plus, those who are the most likely to suffer chronic illness and disabilities. On the basis of a national survey (Factor & Primak, 1990), it was estimated that about 9 percent of Jewish elderly living in the community require at least partial assistance in activities of daily living, whereas this rate among the non-Jewish elderly was close to 23 percent (Barnea & Habib, 1992). Most of the assistance is provided by the family. Only 15 percent of the dependent elderly receive help from public authorities, while 85 percent receive help from informal sources primarily from spouses and children. However, data from a survey of all health and social welfare professionals involved in care planning for the elderly (in three major Israeli cities) reveal that 40 percent of the caregiving families were viewed, or viewed themselves, as being overburdened. In only 30 percent of the cases was it felt that families were able to do more than they were doing (Habib et al., 1988).

In another recent survey in Israel (Brodsky et al., 1991), close to 2,000 elderly and their care providers were interviewed. Table 1 shows that more than 80 percent of the very dependent elders (limited in three or more activities of daily living) live with others (only 17 percent and 15 percent, respectively, live alone); among that group close to 50 percent live with their children (Brodsky, 1991). Data from Table 2 indicate that the burden of care, according to the caregivers, is very heavy. Similar findings on burden of care were presented in a study on the impact of the 1988 Nursing Law on the informal care system (Morginstin & Beitz-Murai, 1992). Close to 50 percent of the children-caregivers studied reported "very

TABLE 1. Selected Characteristics of the Elderly by Dependency Level (percentages).

Dependency Range	Dependent in 1-2 Activities	Dependent in 3-4 Activities	Dependent in 5-6 Activities
	%	%	%
Women	60	57	59
Over 75 years	62	73	67
Over 80 years	41	57	50
Not married	56	46	53
Live alone	28	17	15
Eastern origin	33	52	55
Illiterate	24	40	33
Do not speak Hebrew	22	34	34

TABLE 2. Rate of Individuals Reporting Difficulties in Caregiving, by Difficulty Type and Dependency Level of the Elderly.

Difficulties	Limited in 1-2 Activities	Limited in 3-4 Activities	Limited in 5-6 Acitvities
	%	%	%
Too much pressure	64	93	82
Physical strain	57	75	86
Doing unpleasant tasks	50	70	84
Lack of entertainment	61	84	90
Lack of free time	41	61	53
Tension in supporter family	38	51	36
Emotional difficulties	53	80	63
Do not speak Hebrew	22	34	34

heavy" physical burden and 58 percent reported "very heavy" emotional burden. A third of them reported that they are not coping with the burdens.

One of the outcomes of such ineffective coping was found to be abuse of the care-receivers. It is reasonable to assume that in some of these families there is a potential for incidents of abuse. This assumption was also revealed in a study investigating the relationship between motives for institutionalization of an elderly parent and the parent's impact on family relations (Lowenstein, 1988). In the small sample studied (46 elderly and their caregivers), 12 percent of the families indicated, as one of the major reasons for seeking institutionalization, their fear of becoming abusive towards the elderly parent because they felt that they were being overburdened.

The above data indicate the role strain inherent in the adult child caregiver's role when parent care, employment, and family roles come into conflict. It is especially problematic when a parent moves in with a child as a result of loss of personal resources. The literature shows that caregiver-role overload and confusion, motivation, and deficiencies in skills necessary to care for an elder may be precursors to elder abuse (Zarit, 1980; Brody, 1985; Horowitz,

1985). However, it should be emphasized that most family members provide warm and loving caregiving. In Israel, this love and care are inherent in the Jewish tradition.

One of the ten commandments is: "thou shall honor your father and your mother . . ." (Exodus, 12, 20). The Sages believed that honoring one's parents is even more important than honoring God. Thus, it seems that the Jewish tradition emphasized the normative expectations of familial respect and care to the elderly (Yakovitz, 1983-84). The tradition is manifested in the "obligation principle" of care provision. This principle views the family as obligated to provide care based on its capacity (Habib & Cohen, 1991). It forms the basis for the 1959 Family Law (alimony).

Based on some of the directives of Hebrew law, the Family Law obliges a person to support aged parents (if they cannot support themselves) after meeting the economic needs of the nuclear family and even before an obligation to grown-up children. However, as increasing numbers of elderly require long-term care, and for longer periods of time, the ability and willingness of some families to handle stresses that might result from such prolonged care provision becomes problematic. In certain instances this can lead to abuse of the elderly, in spite of the tradition.

One common problem, for Israel as for other countries, is the lack of firm findings on the prevalence of the problem of maltreatment and the risk factors. An examination of the topology of 29 elder abuse studies revealed that most were based on professional samples, agency data, and studies of awareness of and attitudes to elder abuse (Hudson, 1986). The few research data that exist in Israel are based on some limited professional samples, on a pilot study of the elderly, and on one attitude study.

In a survey of attitudes and perceptions of elder abuse, an urban Israeli sample of 452 people, from different age and ethnic groups, were interviewed. The survey investigated their awareness of the problem, their perceptions of the types of abuse, the severity of the problem, and their knowledge of concrete cases of abuse. The results indicated that 53 percent thought there is "some problem of abuse," while 39 percent thought its scope was wide-spread. Eleven percent knew of at least one case of abuse among friends and relatives, and 7 percent knew about cases of elder abuse within their immediate and extended families (Neikrug et al., 1992).

Elder Abuse Within the "Network of Services"

The interest of Israeli gerontologists in researching the area of elder abuse started while addressing the broader issue of victimization of the aged (Bergman & Amir, 1988; Lowenstein, 1989). One of the major outcomes of this effort was an interdisciplinary international workshop on "Stress, Conflict and Abuse of the Elderly" whose papers were published in a special monograph (Wolf & Bergman, 1989). Elder abuse by formal caregivers in the community, paid helpers caring for a person at home, or semi-professionals and professionals working with the elderly in various community settings is complicated and hard to detect. Since the enactment of the 1988 Nursing Law, which aims at providing nursing home care and personal help to elderly living at home, a larger number of elderly and their families are in contact with paid help. Currently, close to 30,000 elderly are assisted through this law. Such an exposure to lay workers, many of whom have very limited training, might increase the possibility of abuse and neglect. On the other hand, they may, if sensitized to it, be a "discovery agent" of abuse and neglect and report suspected cases of abuse to formal agencies (Lehman, 1989).

One pilot study of fraud against the elderly investigated those who handed over their property and assets to others in return for formal and informal services. The sample was composed of 156 urban aged of European origin living alone (many of whom received compensations from Germany). In addition, data were collected from social workers, nurses, and volunteers who were familiar with the study's sample. The main results indicated that most of the financial abuse of these elderly was by lay helpers who "started" to assist them in order to get access to their financial resources (either in cash or in bank savings). The data showed that 20 percent of the sample had either experienced fraud (8 percent) or were potentially at-risk (12 percent); the latter either not reporting or unaware of it. The researcher proposed a five-stage process of abuse: first, establishing contact and a relationship; second, offering services and help, especially in handling financial affairs; third, increased involvement by the "helper"; fourth, imposing disengagement of the elderly from the outside world; and fifth, disenchantment and disappointment by the elderly. However, even in this final stage, because of the strong needs for companionship of lonely elderly, some were willing "to be defrauded" (Lehman, 1989). No further hard data on this type of abuse are currently available. However, from reports of professionals, this type of abuse seems to be more wide-spread but much harder to detect.

Elder Abuse Within "Residential Settings"

Elder abuse within residential settings is complicated and harder to define and/or detect than abuse within the family or community services. Thus, limited data are presented in the literature about the extent or correlates of abusive behavior of residents (Douglass, 1980; Doty & Sullivan, 1983; Halamandaris, 1983; Long, 1987; Pillemer, 1988; Pillemer & Moore, 1989). The rapid development of the long-term care system in Israel, currently where 19,000 elderly (about 5 percent of those 65 and older) reside in close to 200 facilities, raise interest in studying the quality of care. Within this framework, studies of the quality of life and quality of care of residents also address the issue of elder maltreatment and abuse (Tomer & Fleishman, 1986; Fleishman et al., 1988; Fleishman & Ronen, 1989; Bergman, 1989; Lowenstein & Brick, 1992).

In the study by Fleishman and Ronen (1989), a conceptual framework was presented dealing with two categories of maltreatment: the first, by omission (including passive and active neglect) and the second, by commission (including physical and psychological abuse, violation of rights and liberties, and financial and personal exploitation). In the facilities studied in the report, those which were rated as "poor" by state supervisors had a relatively higher percentage of non-existent or inadequate treatment. For example, acts of omission might refer to a situation in which residents having visual or hearing difficulties would not be seeing a specialist or getting appropriate assistance, thereby limiting their autonomy and social activities. In addition, violation of residents' rights, even to the point of physical and psychological abuse, was observed to be mainly perpetuated by nurses aides. Such abuse included treating the elderly as children, calling them names, shouting, threatening or ignoring their requests.

Social Control Mechanisms

Elder abuse has been the most recent and most neglected form of family violence to vie for public attention in Israel. In the last few years, however, there has been a tightening of social control regarding abuse through special legislation: "The Protection of Helpless Persons (Amendment No. 26 to the Criminal Law), 1989." The law creates a specific social category (helpless) and mandates the professional community to report cases of children and helpless persons, due to age or functioning limitations, who were exposed to abuse. Such a type of legislation sensitizes the society and the formal caregiving system to the phenomenon of elder abuse by focusing on sanctions for and control of the offenders.

The "Protection of the Helpless Law" places the responsibility of reporting on any person witnessing incidents of physical, emotional, or sexual abuse, whether in the community or in a residential facility. If a lay person fails to report, the person might receive three months imprisonment. If a professional fails to do so, the person might get a six months sentence of imprisonment. The maximum penalty for the abuser is a nine year prison sentence.

Welfare officers who are qualified and trained social workers have the major responsibility of initiating a legal procedure through the police and the courts. However, in the regulations of the Law, published by the Ministry of Labour and Social Affairs, the Welfare Officers are directed to use "a treatment" approach when reporting if they think that further harm could be inflicted on the elder.

Under this legislation, the macro-legal system of social control "forces" the professional caregiving community to report and intervene. To provide the workers with adequate tools to enforce the law, a Chief Welfare Officer and Regional Welfare Officers were appointed by the Ministry of Labour and Social Welfare. The enactment of the law encouraged the professionals, and especially the social work community, to start and develop special training programs. A one year course for Welfare Officers was started and, on this basis, a series of workshops was developed (Kerem, 1991/92).

Initially, there was reluctance on the part of practitioners to report and intervene. However, in a recent workshop with 25 social and health care professionals (who were also interviewed), it was found that there was increased awareness of elder abuse which, prior to the enactment of the law, was not considered to be a problem. The professionals' definitions of elder abuse included a strong emphasis on neglect, abandonment, and isolation of the older person from the outside world (in addition to physical and emotional abuse). Most of them could not give estimates of the incidence of abuse. Those who did, though, estimated it to be between 10 to 30 percent. Cases which were brought to their attention, mostly by neighbors or other professionals, included mainly severe neglect and less often physical abuse. Persons at-risk of abuse were either the lonely aged who are exposed to abuse by "outside helpers" or nursing cases who are bound to the home (many of whom suffer from some form of dementia). They were exposed to abuse by their informal caregivers–either a spouse or children (Lowenstein et al., 1992).

To date, two and a half years after the enactment of the law and the regulations, some 80 individual cases of family abuse have been reported to the Chief Welfare Officer (to whom charges are pressed). Moreover, from data gathered by the Ministry of Health, each month at least one case of abuse is reported by many of the 24 general hospitals. In 1992, about 60 cases were reported. However, not all hospitals are reporting on a regular basis and not all cases are diagnosed. It is also not clear how many of these cases are referred to the police or the courts.

The data reported to the Chief Welfare Officer show that a large number of the perpetrators in the community are sons living with, and caring for, an elderly parent–usually a widowed mother who is at least 75. Many of these sons suffer from various mental problems, retardation or other chronic physical and mental conditions. Many are alcohol or drug users. Taking care of the older parent poses a burden the child cannot handle which leads to incidents of abuse. The most common forms of abuse are financial and physical abuse. These data are similar to data by Quinn and Tomita (1986) and Kosberg (1988) that show sons as the main perpetrators of abuse.

The recent enactment of mandatory reporting has helped Welfare Officers to press charges against a small private, for-profit, residential facility. The administrator was charged with excessive abuse of residents and was brought to court. The media played an important role in the administrator's conviction (a sentence of four and a half years imprisonment). The facility was closed by the Ministry of Labor and Social Affairs.

The above information reflects the growing awareness of society and professional caregivers to the phenomenon of elder abuse even though this awareness is still in its infancy stages within Israel. One of the steps to create awareness and to encourage further studies is to start a data base which was undertaken by the Brookdale Institute of Gerontology. A work group was formed which was composed of faculty and researchers from the different universities who are interested in the topic (including social work and health care professionals working with the elderly and representatives of the police). The Ministry of Justice has appointed a special committee to study family violence and abuse. Experts working with the elderly were invited to testify before the committee. The aim was to develop additional legal and social mechanisms to combat problems of abuse within the family setting.

Professional and Ethical Dilemmas

The "Law of Protection of the Helpless" reflects changing directions in the area of social control. But the law also brings to the forefront ethical and professional dilemmas that can be divided into the following three areas: familial norms, personal and cultural perspectives, and professional ethics. In the area of family relations and familial norms, the following dilemmas should be considered: (1) the resistance of elderly clients to use the formal system, especially if it is punitive to their families; (2) the resistance of the elderly to use the system because of certain cultural norms leading to an unwillingness to "wash dirty linen" outside the family network; and (3) the resistance of elderly parents to use the system because of feelings of failure (since they cannot protect their children, however abusive they might be towards them) and their guilt in raising such children.

The dilemmas in the area of personal and cultural norms reflect the heterogeneity of a country that was built on immigration. The main dilemmas are as follows: (1) conflicting societal and ethnic-cultural norms of certain immigrant groups where, for example, wife beating is part of a familial-ethnic culture and is not considered abuse; (2) the reluctance of certain sub-groups among the elderly to be in touch with the formal system (which is considered "the enemy"), where the norm is to "close things" within the extended network; and (3) the existing familial norms of certain groups, where patterns of family violence are a continuation of a 30-40 year life style. Should it be considered as abuse?

In the realm of professional ethics the following are some of the major dilemmas:

1. Mandatory reporting might impact on a client-worker relationship, especially in such a sensitive area as family relations. The issue of confidentiality is very crucial here. Should a treatment or a punitive approach be used?
2. Effective methods of "convincing" an elderly person to press charges against a relative are sometimes difficult to establish. In other words, if an elderly person behaves in a way which suggests adjustment or some form of mistreatment, can it still be considered as abuse and will the professional "convince" the person to report? (This dilemma was also evidenced in relation to the Alimony Law where very few cases were brought to court.)
3. Verbal and/or financial forms of abuse are not included. Should such cases, if detected, be reported or just dealt with in the framework of casework or family therapy?
4. Social workers, in contrast to other professionals such as doctors or nurses, are faced with a potential dilemma. A doctor or a nurse confronted with a case of physical abuse will treat the physical symptoms but will not, usually, be involved with the perpetrator. For the social worker, the situation is different and might impact on willingness to report.
5. Welfare Officers report on the difficulties they encounter in their contact with the police in many regional police departments because they lack trained officers in family relations who have the expertise to investigate such sensitive matters.

The ethical issues of mandatory reporting are directly related to the type of data collected. A comparison of 16 states in the U.S.

revealed a failure to provide consistent information (Salend et al. 1984). Further, it was estimated that although one-third of the actual cases of child abuse is reported, only one out of six cases of elder abuse is reported (U.S. Congress, House Select Committee on Aging, 1980). The main reason is that, unlike the circumstances of small children whose abuse can be detected outside the home, there are no requirements for elderly which necessitate their leaving their homes and, thus, being seen by non-family members.

These are some of the major dilemmas facing the professional caregiving community in Israeli society. These dilemmas will have to be solved so that services and methods of intervention and prevention can be developed.

CONCLUDING REMARKS

This chapter described and analyzed elder abuse in the developing society of Israel. It is evident that the recognition of elder abuse as a social phenomenon is still in its infancy, even more so than in other Western countries. The issues of elder abuse in three environments were discussed: the family setting, formal settings in the community, and in residential facilities. The focus was on the family setting where most care of frail elders takes place. The strong traditional emphasis of the Israeli society on the role of the family as protector of the old might be one of the major reasons for the long delay in recognizing elder abuse as a social problem. This is reflected in the paucity of hard data on the topic and by limited public and professional awareness. Therefore, this chapter used the few available data sources to analyze types of individuals "at risk" of abuse, identify the causes for abuse, and present the main social control mechanisms.

In summary, Israel has undoubtedly entered the "age of aging" (Bergman & Lowenstein, 1988). As the frail elders (and especially the 85 and older group) is expected to grow rapidly, it is reasonable to assume an increase in the incidents of elder abuse in the future. Israel must, therefore, rather urgently address some policy and service issues and map a research agenda. Some specific suggestions can be made:

1. The enactment of the "Protection of the Helpless Law" started a process of sensitization among workers. This process, however, must continue and should be combined with the development of more training programs focusing on detection, prevention and intervention.
2. The issue of elder abuse must be incorporated into the curriculum of professional schools and the teaching of aging.
3. More funds should be allocated for preventive measures including sensitization of the general public, educational programs for caregivers, and more involvement by the media.
4. The criminal justice system should be more open and aware of this issue. Additional channels of communication with the police and the courts need to be developed. As more cases will be brought to court with greater publicity, the public and professionals will need to recognize (and deal with) this phenomenon.
5. Service models and new methods of intervention should be created based on a multidisciplinary approach. The experience from other countries should be studied and adopted to the Israeli culture and milieu.

The research agenda for Israel should include the following areas: (1) developing appropriate definitions and theoretical models appropriate for the Israeli society, (2) developing national and local data bases and carrying out prevalence studies, (3) developing standardized measures of elder abuse, (4) identifying and creating profiles of "at risk" groups in the community and in long-term care settings, and (5) evaluating service models and modes of intervention.

By addressing the issue of elder abuse and recognizing it as a social problem, the quality of life for many Israeli elderly and their families will be enhanced.

REFERENCES

Achdut, L. & Tamir, Y. (1986). *Retirement and well-being among the elderly.* National Insurance Institute, Jerusalem.

Amir, M. & Bergman, S. (1988). *Victimization of the elderly: An analytical review of the literature.* JDC-Brookdale Institute of Gerontology, Jerusalem.

Anetzberger, G. (1987). *The etiology of elder abuse by adult offspring.* Springfield, IL: Charles C Thomas.

Barnea, T. & Habib, J. (Eds.) (1992). *Aging in Israel in the 1990s.* JDC-Brookdale Institute of Gerontology and ESHEL-The Association for the Planning and Development of Services for the Aged in Israel, Jerusalem.

Be'er, S. & Factor, H. (1990). Demographic development of the elderly in Israel in the years 1988-2000. *Gerontology,* 3-21, 47-48. (Hebrew).

Bergman, S. (1980). Israel. In E. Palmore (Ed.) *International handbook on aging.* Westport: Greenwood Press, pp. 208-233.

Bergman, S. & Lowenstein, A. (1988). Care of the aging in Israel: Social service delivery. *Journal of Gerontological Social Work: International Perspectives,* 97-116.

Bergman, S. & Gerstansky, Y. (1989). Promoting the quality of care for psychogeriatric patients. *Social Security, 34,* 99-106. (Hebrew).

Block, M. & Sinnott, J. (Eds.) (1979). *The battered elderly syndrome: An exploratory study.* College Park: Center on Aging, University of Maryland.

Brodsky, J., Sobol, E., Naon, D., King, Y. & Lifshitz, C. (1991). *The functional, health, and social characteristics and needs of the elderly in the community.* JDC-Brookdale Institute of Gerontology, Jerusalem.

Brody, E.M. (1985). Parent care as a normative family stress. *The Gerontologist, 25,* 19-30.

Central Bureau of Statistics. (1989). *Survey of the 60+ in households 1985–Part B: Selected characteristics of the 60+.* Special publications series, no. 840, Jerusalem.

Doty, P & Sullivan, E.W. (1983). Community involvement in combating abuse, neglect, and maltreatment in nursing homes. *Milbank Memorial Fund Quarterly/Health and Society, 61,* 2.

Douglass, R.L. & Hickey, T. (1983). Domestic neglect and abuse of the elderly: Research findings and a systems perspective for service delivery planning. In J.I. Kosberg (Ed.) *Abuse and maltreatment of the elderly: Causes and interventions.* London: John Wright PSG Inc.

Elder abuse. (1992). Senior NCNS, South African Council on Aging.

Factor, H. & Primak, H. (1990). *Dependency amongst the aged in Israel.* Discussion paper: D-180-90. JDC-Brookdale Institute of Gerontology, Jerusalem.

Fleishman, R. & Tomer, A. et al. (1986). *Evaluation of quality of care in longterm care institutions in Israel: The tracer approach.* Discussion Paper: D-125-86, JDC-Brookdale Institute of Gerontology, Jerusalem.

Fleishman, R. & Ronen, R. (1989). Quality of care and maltreatment in Israel's institutions for the elderly. In R.S. Wolf & S. Bergman (Eds.) *Stress, conflict and abuse of the elderly.* JDC-Brookdale Institute of Gerontology, Jerusalem.

Fleishman, R., Bar-Giora, M., Ronen, R., Mandelson, J. & Bentley, L (1990). Improving quality of care in Israel's long-term care institutions. *World Health Forum, 9*(3), 327-335.

Girodano, N.H. & Giordano, J.A. (1984). Elder abuse: A review of the literature. *Social Work, 29*(3), 232-236.

Guttmann D. & Lowenstein, A. (forthcoming). The graying of Israel. In Olson (Ed.) *The graying of the world.*

Habib, J., Factor, H., Naon, D., Brodsky, E. & Dolev, T. (1988). *Disabled elderly in the community: Developing adequate community-based services and their implications for the need for institutional placement, stage two: Evaluation by multidisciplinary teams.* Discussion paper: d-160-88, JDC-Brookdale Institute of Gerontology, Jerusalem.

Habib, J. & Cohen, M. (1991). *Strategies for addressing the needs of the very old.* JDC-Brookdale Institute of Gerontology, Jerusalem.

Halamandaris, V. (1983). Fraud and abuse in nursing homes. In J.I. Kosberg (Ed.) *Abuse and maltreatment of the elderly: Causes and interventions.* London: John Wright, PSG Inc.

Horowitz, A. & Shnidelman, L.W. (1983). Reciprocity and affection: Past influences on current caregiving. *Journal of Gerontological Social Work, 5*(3), 5-20.

Horowitz, A. (1985). Sons and daughters as caregivers to older parents: Differences in role performance and consequences. *The Gerontologist, 25*(6), 612-617.

Hudson, M.F. (1986). Elder mistreatment: Current research. In K.A. Pillemer & R.S. Wolf (Eds.) *Elder Abuse: Conflict in the family.* Dover, MA: Auburn House.

Kerem, B.Z. (1991/92). *Abuse of the helpless elderly.* Newsletter of the Israeli Gerontological Association, No. 82. (Hebrew).

Kosberg, J.I. (1983). The special vulnerability of elderly parents. In J.I. Kosberg (Ed.) *Abuse and maltreatment of the elderly: Causes and interventions.* London: John Wright, PSG Inc.

Kosberg, J.I. (1988). Preventing elder abuse: Identification of high risk factors prior to placement decisions. *The Gerontologist, 28*(1), 43-50.

Lau, E.E. & Kosberg, J.I. (1979). Abuse of the elderly by informal care providers. *Aging,* 10-15.

Lehman, H. (1989). Fraud and abuse of the elderly. In R.S. Wolf & S. Bergman (Eds.) *Stress, conflict and abuse of the elderly.* JDC-Brookdale Monograph series, Jerusalem.

Long, S. (1987). *Death without dignity.* Austin, TX: Texas Monthly Press.

Lowenstein, A. (1989). *Institutional placement decision-making and impact on family relations of the elderly–A filial crisis.* Paper presented at the Annual Symposium of the European Behavioral and Social Science Research Section of the International Association of Gerontology, Dubrovnick, Yugoslavia.

Lowenstein, A. (1989). The elderly victim and the welfare services. In R.S. Wolf & S. Bergman (Eds.) *Stress, conflict and abuse of the elderly.* JDC-Brookdale Institute of Gerontology, Jerusalem.

Lowenstein, A., Bergman, S. & Schwartz, V. (1992). *Elder abuse in a forming society.* Paper presented at the Annual Symposium of the European Behavioral and Social Science Research Section of the International Association of Gerontology, Bratislava, Slovakia.

Lowenstein, A. & Brick, Y. (1992). *Quality of life in residential settings in Israel.* Paper presented at the Annual Symposium of the European Behavioral and Social Science Research section of the International Association of Gerontology, Bratislava, Slovakia.

Morginstin, B. & Cohen S. (1980). Shared living of the elderly with married sons. *Gerontology*, 39-48. (Hebrew).

Morginstin, B. (1990). *The impact of demographic and socioeconomic factors on the changing needs of the very old.* Discussion Paper 3. National Insurance Institute, Jerusalem.

Morginstin, B. & Beitz-Morai, S. (1992). *The impact of the Nursing Law on the informal support network of dependent elderly.* National Insurance Institute, Jerusalem, Survey N. 92. (Hebrew).

Neikrug, S., Ronen, M. Edelstein et al., (1992). *Abuse of the elderly in Israel.* Unpublished manuscript, Bar Ilan University, Ramat Gan.

Noam, G. (1989). *Kinship networks of the elderly.* JDC-Brookdale Institute of Gerontology, Jerusalem.

O'Malley, H., Segars, H., Perex, R. et al. (1979). *Elder abuse in Massachusetts: A survey of professionals and paraprofessionals.* Boston: Legal Research and Services for the Elderly.

Pillemer, K. & Wolf, R.S. (1986). *Elder abuse: Conflict in the family.* Dover, MA: Auburn House.

Pillemer, K. & Finkelhor, D. (1988). The prevalence of elder abuse: A random sample survey. *The Gerontologist, 28*(1), 51-57.

Pillemer, K. (1988). Maltreatment of patients in nursing homes: Overview and research agenda. *Journal of Health and Social Behavior, 28,* 227-238.

Pillemer, K. & Moore, D.W. (1989). Abuse of patients in nursing homes: Findings from a survey of staff. *The Gerontologist, 29*(3), 314-320.

Poertner, J. (1986). Estimating the incidence of abused elder persons. *Journal of Gerontological Social Work, 9*(3), 3-15.

Quinn, M.J. & Tomita, S.K. (1986). *Elder abuse and neglect.* New York: Springer.

Rathbone-McCuan, E. (1980). Elderly victims of family violence and neglect. *Social Casework,* 296-304.

Sabatello, E.F. (1989). Chosen demographic indicators to aging process of the Israeli population till 2025. *Gerontology,* 22-23, 43-44. (Hebrew).

Salend, E., Kane, R.A., Satz, M. & Pynoos, J. (1984). Elder abuse reporting: Limitation of statutes. *The Gerontologist, 24,* 61-69.

Sengstock, M.C. & Liang, J. (1982). *Identifying and characterizing elder abuse.* Detroit: Wayne State University, Institute of Gerontology.

Shmueli, A. (1989). Single and multi-generational living arrangements of elderly persons in Israel, 1972-1982. *Social Security, 33,* 32-43. (Hebrew).

Shmueli, A. (1989). *Kinship networks in Israel.* JDC-Brookdale Institute of Gerontology, Jerusalem.

Shuval, J., Fleishman, R. & Shmueli, A. (1982). *Informal support of the elderly.* JDC-Brookdale Institute of Gerontology, Jerusalem.

Steinmetz, S.K. (1983). Dependency, stress and violence between middle-aged caregivers and their elderly parents. In J.I. Kosberg (Ed.) *Abuse and maltreatment of the elderly: Causes and interventions.* London: John Wright, PSG, Inc.

Steinmetz, S.K. (1988). *Duty bound: Elder abuse and family care.* Berkeley Hills, CA: Sage.

Tomlin, S. (1989). *Abuse of the elderly people: An unnecessary and preventable problem.* London: The British Geriatrics Society.

U.S. Congress, House Select Committee on Aging. (1981). *Elder abuse: The hidden problem.* Washington, DC: Government Printing Office.

U.S. Congress, House Select Committee on Aging. (1985). *Elder abuse: A national disgrace.* Washington, DC: Government Printing Office.

Wolf, R.S., Strugnell, C.P. & Godkin, M.A. (1982). *Preliminary findings from three model projects on elder abuse.* Worcester, MA: University of Massachusetts Medical Center.

Wolf, R.S. (1986). Major findings from three model projects on elder abuse. In K.A. Pillemer & R.S. Wolf (Eds.) *Elder abuse: Conflict in the family.* Dover, MA: Auburn House.

Wolf, R.S. & Bergman, S. (1989). *Stress, conflict, and abuse of the elderly.* JDC-Brookdale Institute of Gerontology, Jerusalem.

Yacovitz, E. (1983-84). The responsibility of adult children for their old parents. *Gerontology,* 25-26, 28-38. (Hebrew).

Young, R.F. & Kahana, E. (1989). Specifying caregiver outcomes: Gender and relationship aspects of caregiving strain. *The Gerontologist,* 29, 660-676.

Zarit, S.H., Reever, K.E. & Back-Peterson, J. (1980). Relatives of the impaired elderly: Correlates of feelings of burden. *The Gerontologist,* 20, 649-655.

Zilberstein, Y. (1981). *Medical and social needs of dependent elders–Needed services and their costs.* National Insurance Institute, Jerusalem. (Hebrew).

Chapter 7

Elder Abuse in India

Gita Shah, PhD
Rosamma Veedon, MSW
Sabiha Vasi, MSW

. . . a silent revolution, a coup of sorts is taking place. The patriarch, the matriarch, the eldest son, the aging boss, and the village elder are being elbowed aside. The youth are moving in. Children are even throwing their parents out. (Jain & Menon, 1991, 47)

These words aptly describe the Indian situation on aging. The gerontocracy that dominated most spheres of human activity, whether it be political, social, economic, or family is being forced to vacate and make way for the younger generation. This, at times, is smooth, at times, painful, and at times, violent resulting in either physical, financial, or psychological abuse of the aging.

Physical acts of violence causing injury and pain to the elderly do not seem to be common; however, abandonment and neglect are rather widespread. This is an unfortunate development, since traditionally such treatment towards the elderly was rare, because of the

Gita Shah is Head, Department of Extra Mural Studies, Tata Institute of Social Sciences, Deonar, Bombay 400 088, India. Rosamma Veedon is Lecturer, Unit for Family Studies and Sabiha Vasi is Faculty Assistant, Department of Extra Mural Studies, both at the Tata Institute.

[Haworth co-indexing entry note]: "Elder Abuse in India." Shah, Gita, Rosamma Veedon, and Sabiha Vasi. Co-published simultaneously in the *Journal of Elder Abuse & Neglect* (The Haworth Press, Inc.) Vol. 6, No. 3/4, 1995, pp. 101-118; and: *Elder Abuse: International and Cross-Cultural Perspectives* (ed: Jordan I. Kosberg, and Juanita L. Garcia) The Haworth Press, Inc., 1995, pp. 101-118. Multiple copies of this article/chapter may be purchased from The Haworth Document Delivery Center [1-800-3-HAWORTH; 9:00 a.m. - 5:00 p.m. (EST)].

conservative Indian ethos emphasizing reciprocity and interdependence at an intergenerational level. Since the family and the community fulfilled everyone's need of sustenance, there was no necessity for a formal social security mechanism. This built-in system of ancient and medieval India is eroding in modern times.

GENERAL OVERVIEW OF AGING IN INDIA

Population Size. India, like most countries of the world, is witnessing a demographic transition. The aging population (those above the age of 60) is increasing both in terms of number as well as in proportion to the general population. Being the second most populous country in the world, the number of older Indians is substantial: 55 million and 6.5 percent of the total population according to the 1991 census. The average life span has risen to 58 years as compared to 32 years in 1947. Further, Gokhale and Dave (1992) report that the number of old in absolute terms is likely to rise to 76.5 million by the turn of the century as compared to 43 million in 1981.

Religious Stratification. A majority of Indians follow Hinduism. However, other religions like Buddhism, Christianity, Islam, Jainism, and Sikhism co-exist.

Residence. An estimated 39.45 million elderly live in rural areas as compared to 8.75 million in urban areas (National Sample Survey, July 1986 to June 1987).

Marital Status. A large number of women in the age group of 60 plus are widowed. They, along with the never-married and divorced, constitute two-thirds of all females in the 60 plus age group in 1981 as compared to only about one-fifth of the males in these categories (Bose, 1992).

Elder Employment. Most of the elderly men, particularly in the rural areas, continue to be economically active, since mandatory retirement is applicable only in the organized sector of employment which comprises less than one-tenth of the total Indian work force. Between July 1986 and June 1987, the percentage of employed elderly men in rural areas was 59.2, and that of elder women, 12.8. In urban areas the percentage of employed elderly was 41.3 for men and 5.9 for women during the same period (Gokhale & Dave, 1992).

Those working in the unorganized sector include persons belonging to the lower income groups, generally involved in unskilled labor as well as affluent individuals managing their private enterprises. While persons who have retired from the organized sector are provided with a certain amount of economic security through provisions like the provident fund, pensions, and gratuity, those belonging to the unorganized sector do not share such benefits.

Educational Status. Literacy in the population 60 plus for both males and females is much lower than in the general population: 34.6 percent for males and 7.8 percent for females (Bose, 1992).

The above statistics project a general overview of the elderly in India. However, many differences exist, especially in terms of culture, language, and religion. Further, the impact of developmental efforts has not been uniform. In this respect, some parts of the country are comparable to developed countries in terms of literacy, mortality, growth rate, and status of women, while other parts of the country are far below the world average.

ELDER ABUSE

Definitions

In this chapter, elder abuse is defined as infliction of physical, mental, and financial power on the aging resulting in loss of their rights. A review of literature in *Aged and the Family* by Desai, Bharat, and Veedon (1993) reflects the absence of any research or published material on elder abuse in India. One cannot say that elder abuse is very prevalent in India, although its presence is felt. This is reflected in available records of social work practitioners and of institutions for the aging as well as in films, plays, and creative literature. Different types of abuse include physical violence, threatening behavior, neglect and abandonment, financial exploitation, and psychological torment.

Nature of Elder Abuse in India

Violence in the home and abuse of family members who are less capable of defending themselves such as women, children, the handicapped, and the elderly has always existed. In India, since age is venerated, the elderly are still treated with a certain amount of respect and thus not consciously singled out for direct abuse. Unfortunately, this conservatism is undergoing a metamorphosis in both urban and rural areas. Technological innovations and modernization are bringing about a materialistic, individualistic, and impersonalized lifestyle. Migration, an indicator of development, is one factor that has had unfavorable consequences for both the urban and rural elderly, but in different ways.

In India it is difficult to categorize any specific abuse. Financial, physical, and psychological abuse, as well as neglect and abandonment, are interlinked when one examines the scenario of elder abuse in India. This condition is substantiated by the following examples.

Financial Abuse

In respect to crimes committed against elderly citizens, I.U. Khan, a criminal lawyer of New Delhi reports that:

> fifty percent of such crimes in Delhi city involve family members because of inheritance problems. The aged, at times, threaten to disinherit their children who sometimes hire killers. Others force them to hand over property, and then abandon them in old age homes. Migration has resulted in a large number of elderly living alone. (cited by Jain & Menon, 1991, 51)

An article in the *Times of India* newspaper reported still another instance of such crime committed against the elderly:

> Mr. A.S.B. (75) and his wife, who set up a successful chain of schools in Chandigarh city, were defrauded of their property by their own son. Once prosperous, they are now reduced to living in an institution. (*Daily*, 1991, 13)

Physical Abuse

Abandonment of elderly family members as well as their banishment to special homes for the aging is an event that is being noticed, especially since–culturally–institutionalization of the elderly is an alien concept in India. Its occurrence, hence, indicates a dysfunction in the familial and societal mechanisms and safeguards that have almost proverbially existed in the Indian family system for providing care to the aging. Hospital social workers have recounted that many elderly are 'dumped' in hospitals without accurate information regarding their residential address.

The reasons for such treatment are complex. One of the explanations pertains to a lack of preparedness of the respective family members to shoulder the 'burden' of looking after their aging relative(s), especially if the latter is/are ailing or in need of special attention and care. The 'burden' is perceived in terms of resources expended, essentially time and money. On the other hand, investment of these same resources in younger members of the family, especially children, tends to be viewed as more productive and worthwhile.

The following instances, reported in the daily newspapers, describe the nature of ill-treatment in India. Social work agency records also cast light upon this subject.

> Mrs. X a Christian widow, suffering from diabetes and high blood-pressure, was being physically abused by her younger alcoholic son with the intention of usurping her residential one-room apartment. The elder son staying in a far-off suburb did not find time to reach out and help her. The police, too, were reluctant to intervene and protect Mrs. X as the problem was a domestic one. She was hence persuaded to join a 'Day-Care Center.' Lack of family support and over-crowded public transport added to her difficulties in availing of medical assistance. (Case Record, Family Welfare Agency, Bombay)

This case illustration clearly is an example of physical abuse and non-availability of support from the family, professionals, and law enforcement representatives. Increasingly, the aged are being discarded by the young as soon as they have usurped their property.

> After Mr. A (60) was found on a garbage heap in Madras he was taken to an institution. His family soon turned up to retrieve him—but only till he was made to sign off his 10 acre property. Then, it was back to the streets. Similarly, Ms. L.

(84) was bundled off to an institution in Madras by her children when her husband died after being forced to relinquish her property. (Jain & Menon, 1991, 50)

Neglect

Closely related to this issue of abandonment is that of neglect. This type of mistreatment is generally manifested in less severe forms of ill-treatment, like insensitivity and negligence towards the needs of the elderly. For instance, Mr. B. (81), who retired as a grocer and now lives with his married daughter in Bombay, laments, "I am not ill-treated but they do not care for me either. I am an outsider here. I am always excluded" (*Daily*, 1992, 13).

Ms. G., a widow and mother of five children, lives with her married son along with her unmarried children. According to Ms. G's report, her daughter-in-law used to prepare the daily meals for the entire family, but, of late, she (Ms. G.) had started cooking meals for herself and her unmarried off-spring, separately. Further inquiry indicated that Ms. G. was unhappy with her daughter-in-law's attitude while serving the food, which she described as, 'she (daughter-in-law) serves food like throwing left overs to the dogs.' Presently, Ms. G. puts up with all difficulties and continues to stay with her son as she cannot afford to rent a separate house and moreover, she is at the mercy of her son and his wife to get the other children married. (Mary, N.D.)

Another case reported by Mehta (1992) demonstrates the predicament of an elderly widow (80) living with her son and his family.

When Ms. R.'s husband was alive she enjoyed all the luxuries of life–a large bungalow to live in, abundant domestic help, land, property and other assets. Soon after losing her husband, her son sold off their property and usurped all the family's savings in the bank. The family then shifted from the large bungalow to a small apartment in a building.
  Presently this old lady gets almost nothing to eat from her daughter-in-law. She survives on tea and buttermilk, but cov-

ers up for this by saying, 'I cannot digest anything else.' She is also not allowed to turn on the fan, use the geyser or gas stove. However, she is expected to do all the washing and make 8 cups of tea every morning for all the family members, even though she cannot stand upright or hold the heavy and hot tea pot. She is relegated to a room at the back of the house and is not permitted to leave it. She is also prevented from entertaining visitors or making visits. If relatives drop in by chance, her daughter-in-law does not let them out of her sight. Her son supports his wife's behavior and does nothing to ameliorate his mother's condition. Ms. R. never complains about her predicament and hence relatives and well-wishers are ignorant about her situation. Whenever news of relatives/friends passing away is received, Ms. R. reacts by saying, 'Oh dear! It was my turn to go, why has God not taken me instead of him/her?'

This case reflects a combination of abusive behavior towards an elderly widow. The situation described above might not have arisen at all if Ms. R.'s husband had been alive. Non-assertiveness exhibited by Ms. R. is self-induced abuse and the expression of a desire to die indicates deep rooted sorrow accompanied by covert psychological torment.

The problem of neglect has been further intensified in India by large-scale migration of the young and able-bodied from rural to urban centers as well as to other countries. Consequently, the elderly are left behind to fend for themselves. It has been reported that when the young of tribal populations migrate to nearby towns or cities in search of jobs, they leave their old folk behind. The elderly, hence, have to fend for themselves in geographical areas where there is a scarcity of resources.

Another current example are the elderly women living alone and earning their livelihood by doing domestic work in affluent households. With the migration of their sons abroad, they have to sustain themselves. Some were injured during the recent riots in Bombay and lost their jobs which was their only means of income. Even in this situation of dire need, their migrated offspring neglected them by not offering aid of any kind. Financial assistance from migrated children is often lacking and/or inadequate.

Leela (80) says she feels like an aimless wanderer going around her village in search of some odd job. Her three sons are away in Delhi and they have their own children to look after, she rationalizes! (Jain & Menon, 1991, 50)

Emotional or Psychological Abuse

Abuse at the psychological level is far more pervasive, although hidden. It occurs in varying ways, such as (1) being taken for granted, (2) being used as additional domestic help, (3) not being included in the family's social events, (4) being made the focus of cruel jokes of youngsters, and (5) not being acknowledged or appreciated for contributions made in household chores, especially with many young women working outside the household. A male resident of a Clergy Home in Bombay city captures, succinctly, feelings of bitterness and hurt towards the younger generation. He alludes to the world being peopled by those without "ethics or conscience." Whenever he steps out, he says, young boys and girls mock him. "They fool me by calling me 'Padre, Padre' and then throw pebbles at me. At times like this I feel old and neglected."

Some of the Indian dramas and films depict psychological abuse very aptly. For example, a Marathi play entitled, "Natsamrat" depicts the plight of old parents who initially had to shift residence from one son's home to another. Later on, they were separated to suit the convenience of their sons. Soon after, their children refused to give them any shelter and relegated them to an outhouse. Then, the old couple was confronted with a situation where they were accused of stealing money from one of their son's home. This dramatic portrayal reflects the emerging attitude of younger children towards old parents (*Daily*, 1991, 51).

Financial Abuse

Subjection of senior family members to the psychological trauma of implicating them as insane in order to gain control of their financial assets is not an uncommon practice. The following illustrations, quoted from a newspaper article, bears testimony to such situations.

Ms. V. (67), a widow, is currently an inmate of an old age home in Bombay city. Her late husband had willed his property and savings to her. Being educated, she managed her own financial affairs. However, gradually after his death her sons began pressuring her to transfer the assets to their name. However, she refused to comply which led to conflict and tension all around. As this situation worsened, feelings of insecurity, suspiciousness, and fear intensified, especially in the absence of a sympathetic ear to share her troubles. In a desperate bid to take over their mother's wealth, Ms. V.'s sons conspired in declaring her insane of mind and hospitalized her for treatment. Returning from the hospital she was once again harassed and finally forced to move into a home for the aged as she stuck to her position and wanted to retain her financial assets. She still lives in the hope of going back home, someday.

Mrs. Z. was informally adopted for board and lodging by a young couple. The arrangement was that this couple would accommodate Mrs. Z. in their house after they bought it at a very nominal rate. Mrs. Z. thus paid a small rent of Rs. 50/per month. Sometime there after Mrs. Z. inherited Rs. 17,000/ after which trouble with her adopted family began. The young couple started making additional monetary demands upon her. To get respite from this situation she moved in with her stepdaughter. However, here too she faced a similar problem and thus had to move back to living with her adopted family. (Case Records, Family Welfare Agency, Bombay)

The above cases clearly indicate harassment of the elderly (especially women) for financial reasons.

Self-Induced Abuse

Data are not readily available on self-induced abuse, as many of these cases are often not perceived as acts of self-directed violence and, therefore, do not get reported or documented. Consequently, agency records do not include such cases. However, articles in newspapers and magazines, as well as research studies, throw some light onto cases of self-induced abuse of the elderly. In this connection, a case is reported of an old lady living in a village who broke her own leg out of frustration at her loneliness (*Times of India,* August 17, 1992, 13). The rise in the actual suicide rate (and attempts at suicide) among the elderly is evident. The putative causes are social isolation, economic desperation, and psychiatric disorders. The latter is comprised mainly of depression which is more often precipitated by life events, with social implications rather than endogenous factors (Venkoba Rao, 1985).

To summarize, the exact extent and nature of the different kinds of elder abuse presently prevalent in India is difficult to gauge due to lack of adequate research studies. A review of newspaper reports and news items, one manner of identifying instances of elder abuse, is largely confined to accounts in urban India–while rural India constitutes 65 percent of the population.

SUBGROUPS OF ELDERLY AT RISK OF ABUSE

Persons hailing from differing income groups as well as elderly women have been considered at special risk of abuse.

Elder Abuse and the Socioeconomic Status of the Elderly

Elderly belonging to the lower socioeconomic strata largely fall into the unorganized sector, where physical and unskilled labor is the predominant means of livelihood. In such a situation, advancing age takes its toll in terms of decreasing one's ability to engage in arduous labor and, finally, forcing one to drop out of the labor market. This is coupled with a marked absence of any personal financial security due to abject poverty. These factors contribute to creating a total dependency (especially economic) of the aged on their young offspring/relatives for sustenance. This dependency curtails the decision-making power of elderly persons within their respective family units. As a result, they undergo much stress and strain. Intrafamily tensions and acrimonious scenes between the elderly and their offspring thus ensue. A feeling of being rejected leads to a depressed mood and a sense of worthlessness among the aged (Miranda, 1992, 3-5).

It is clear that in such a situation, senior family members are almost totally at the mercy of their more able-bodied counterparts and are thus susceptible to abuse in the form of abandonment, neglect, and coercion to do domestic chores, including baby sitting for their grandchildren. This is compounded by space (housing) constraints faced by the family, especially in slum communities. On the other hand, businesspersons and professionals, by virtue of possessing considerable wealth, are placed at a high risk of being subjected to financial abuse. Attempts to defraud them and usurp their wealth are likely to occur. Retirees, in the organized sector, too, may be subject to such an ordeal.

Elder Abuse and Women

Abuse of elderly women is not only rampant in India but also cuts across all age groups and exists at all levels: *formal* (education, employment, etc.) and *informal* (marriage, family relationships, etc.). The impact of old age on women is different from that on men because of the differences in their status and role in society. The unfavorable and patronizing attitude of the Indian society towards the female sex does not spare aging women. Women are considered to be dependents (on their husbands, offspring/relatives) throughout life, with old age no exception. This dependency is further intensified by the presence of a high level of illiteracy, a lack of remunerative occupation, as well as negligible awareness about legal and economic rights among elderly women in comparison to their male counterparts. Dependency, along with the onset of a changing lifestyle from traditional to modern, compounds the problems faced by elderly women, whether single, married, widowed, divorced, or childless.

In the traditional life cycle of Indian women, there existed considerable contrast between their role as wife and mother. The position of a wife was one of subordination, but that of a mother was one of power. It is through her status as a mother that a woman was able to ameliorate her position as a wife. As a mother, she controlled the socialization of children, ran the household, and later controlled her daughter-in-law. However, in recent times, a number of factors, mainly high levels of literacy amongst the younger generation (male and female), the onset of an individualistic and materialistic outlook on life and the generation of new interests and ideals have contributed in altering the position, role and status of elderly women within their respective family units.

Thus, older women who have been longing to play the authoritative role of mother-in-law find that the role is meaningless in the context of the new, contemporary world of working women. The center of power is no longer the mother-in-law; this results in making them feel less important. The working women's situation, consequently, introduces growing incompatibility in interests and expectations between the young and the old, pertaining to matters of conjugal relationships, child rearing, and home management. Interpersonal conflicts further aggravate the already tense state of affairs. Physical and financial dependence on one's family only worsens the predicament of older women, especially if widowed. The situation becomes more difficult for elderly widows when sons decide to move out of the extended family pattern and set up nuclear units of their own. Such instances result in not only rejection and neglect, but can lead to theft, robbery, and sometimes even murder of these helpless, old women living by themselves. Besides, psychological trauma arising out of loneliness and desperation runs deep.

Thus, in India, women's high dependency status creates many difficulties for elderly women. This factor along with the physiological helplessness experienced, as a direct consequence of their advancing age and decreasing capabilities, contribute to placing elderly women at a higher risk of being abused.

THE CAUSES OF ELDER ABUSE IN INDIA

Financial and psychological abuse seem to be far more prevalent than physical abuse in India. One of the reasons why physical abuse is rare is because age is still venerated and societal pressure against individuals who abuse their parents or other elderly members is still strong. 'Ageism' is not as common as in the West, mainly because the elderly receive very few benefits from the government. They are still dependent on themselves and their family members. The situation of a middle-aged daughter having to continuously provide care for an aged parent, as in the West, is not common in India. Often the caregiving role is shared by all the members of the family and so the family's coping capacity is greater.

However, when it comes to the financial situation, many of the elderly, schooled in the traditional beliefs that they have to give up their worldly goods and prepare themselves for the next, become easy victims of financial exploitation. According to the Hindu tradition, the life cycle is divided into four stages, the first two deal with childhood and adulthood, *'brahmacharya'* and *'gruhastha'* while the last two deal with aging. *'Vanaprasthashrama,'* 'vana' (forest) 'prastha' (living in) 'ashrama' (period of)–a stage for preparing to live a life of detachment in the forests along with one's spouse, and *'Sanyasahrama,'* 'sanyasa' (complete renunciation of the world, its possessions and attachments) and 'ashrama' (period of)–leading the life of a hermit. Many elderly persons willingly or at the suggestion of the younger members give away all their wealth to their sons, in the hope that they will be looked after as they themselves had looked after their parents. But with changing times, materialism and individualism have made inroads into Indian society. Consequently, offspring may migrate to cities or sell-off the property they have inherited without discharging their responsibilities toward their parents.

In spite of all the cultural pressure for respecting the elderly and caring for them, there is also a certain amount of a callousness and apathy towards providing services for those who are suffering or in need. This neglect results mainly from the belief in the 'Karma' theory, according to which all the suffering that one undergoes in this life is due to sins committed in one's previous life, of which widowhood is considered to be the greatest punishment.

The contemporary Indian society is also witnessing a decline in the status of the elderly. According to Bose (1992), some of the factors that have contributed to this are as follows:

- Decline in the institution of the family and weakening of the roles that elderly people were traditionally expected to play in matters concerning the extended family, caste and the village.
- Greater vulnerability among the elderly due to fewer children to depend on, especially with the acceptance of a small family norm in the middle and upper classes of society.

- A reduction in the caregiving role provided by women due to greater employment opportunities available for them particularly in the cities.
- Migration of younger members to the cities in search of employment leaving the elderly behind in the villages to fend for themselves.
- Acute paucity of accommodations in urban areas, exorbitant rents and high living costs which act as strong disincentives to bring old parents to live with them.
- Economic dependency among the elderly due to absence of old age security benefits.

These factors have also contributed to the increased vulnerability of the elderly to exploitation by family members and society. Explanations for the causes of elder abuse in India may be viewed from two perspectives: the traditional Indian philosophy of life and the impact of modernization. A combination of both these perspectives must be considered in understanding the nature and extent of elder abuse currently prevalent in India.

EFFORTS TO INTERVENE IN THE PROBLEM OF ELDER ABUSE

Elder abuse has received very little attention in India and so there are no specific policies, programs, and services in this area. However, in some states there are old age pension schemes for indirectly preventing, detecting, and intervening in the problem of elder abuse. Government and voluntary organizations can initiate efforts. Legislation makes it a responsibility of children to look after their aging parent(s). According to Section 125 of the code of criminal procedure, 1973, all persons (male or female), with sufficient means, have to maintain their parents who are unable to maintain themselves. This provision is in addition to Section 29(3) of the Hindu Adoption and Maintenance Act, 1956, which makes it obligatory on the part of a person to maintain his or her aging, infirm parents. In spite of these legal provisions, it is very seldom that parents sue their children for maintenance.

There have been publicity efforts, through newspaper articles and the media, to educate older people about the need to be cautious about giving away all their wealth to their children during their lifetime because, in the current period of transition, they cannot rely on the traditional support system.

Non-governmental organizations are playing a pioneering role in providing services and meeting welfare needs of the elderly. Some of the services include the provision of mobile geriatric care, establishment of supplementary feeding and health check-ups, organization of daycare centers, sponsorship of elderly in foster families, dissemination of information on planning for retirement, setting up of old age homes wherever necessary, and formation of self-help groups.

The role of the government has been mainly that of providing financial assistance to non-governmental organizations working with the elderly. The subject of aging is the responsibility of the state government, and they provide pensions to the destitute old. The pension provided is very meager and covers only a small proportion of all destitute elderly persons.

FUTURE PROJECTS

It is difficult to predict the status of elder abuse in India because of the lack of empirical data. The extent of the problem hinges upon various changes that are currently taking place in the country. These changes may be viewed from a macro- and micro-level.

Macro-Level Changes

Privatization of Services. Changes in the current economic policies indicate a move towards privatization of services such as specialized health care and higher education that could affect the elderly in indirect ways, leading to increased abuse. The aging in India require specialized health services which, if privatized, will incur considerable expenditure. This increased monetary expense may act as a disincentive (an added economic burden on resources, especially in the absence of any social security measures) for families in attending to the health needs of the aged. Transportation costs, in terms of money and time spent in accompanying the elderly to the medical centers, might act as another disincentive. In such a situation, abuse of the elderly through neglecting their health needs may increase.

In India, substantial importance is given to higher, specialized education by the upper- and middle-classes of society. Parents tend to give priority to their offsprings' education over satisfaction of their own requirements. Privatization of advanced and specialized education would once again lead to increased financial expenditure for the family. Thus, in the light of the above-mentioned parental disposition, it is only obvious that the family's resources will get channelled in favor of educational opportunities for the young. In the bargain, the needs of the elderly will be compromised and thus neglect will occur once again.

Housing and Migration. Adequate shelter/housing is one of the major problems facing the country. In recent times, the number of poor people living in slums has risen to 50 million (a quarter of India's urban population). This situation will take its toll on the elderly by depriving them of private floor space in the house (lack of privacy) and also make them vulnerable to financial abuse for transference of their property and holdings. Increasing migration of the youth to cities, in search of better employment opportunities, will also lead to abandonment and neglect.

Micro-Level Changes

A few studies show that (1) in spite of modernization and urbanization, familial and filial bondages are not disrupted to a significant extent (Ramamurthi & Jamuna, 1986); (2) intergenerational antipathy between the old and the young is due more to differences in interest rather than in values (Ramamurthi, Kullai, & Reddy, 1986; (3) failure on the part of sons to look after their old parents is still considered a serious demerit and earns social disapproval (D'Souza, 1982), and (4) family and kin still play an important role in providing economic and social security to the aging (Desai & Naik, 1971; Vatuk, 1980). Traditional values and filial piety are too much a part of the Indian ethos to be given up easily. However, the influence of developmental changes on this outlook is difficult to predict.

It is still probable that the elders may be abused financially due to increased materialism, abandoned in situations of extreme poverty, and physically abused in situations of substance abuse. It is also probable that the abuse of the elderly may result from a general increase of violence in the society, but the possibility of the elderly being singled out for abuse does not seem likely to increase.

The above discussion clearly indicates that the aged form a population at risk of abuse. However, at the same time, efforts are being directed to overcome this situation. For instance, media (films, dramas, newspaper/magazine articles), professionals, and the aged themselves are currently playing an active role in sensitizing both the general public as well as the elderly themselves regarding the needs, problems, and rights of the aging. The emergence of self-help groups in the recent past is another example of awareness-building among the elderly regarding their rights. Such self-help groups serve to enable the elderly to become more assertive by drawing support from their peers. The organized sector is contributing in this direction by offering its employees training in 'retirement planning.' The major emphasis of such training is on economic planning. The government of India, too, has developed schemes to help young people in planning for old age. Finally, the Indian ethos encapsulates the idea of duty towards the elderly at the individual and societal levels. Thus, the elderly might be abused to a lesser degree.

In sum, it is difficult to predict the prevalence and occurrence of elder abuse, as India is currently at the crossroads between tradition and modernization. The future trends of elder abuse will thus depend upon the manner in which the country copes with this situation. However, with growing sensitization of the public, professionals in the field as well as the elderly themselves, concentrated efforts to detect, analyze, and counter elder abuse are likely to be undertaken in the near future.

REFERENCES

Bose, A.B. (1992). *Country report: India.* Paper presented at the International Federation on Ageing–First Global Conference, Bombay, Aug.-Sept.

D'Souza, V.S. (1982). *The aged in India.* Paper presented at the World Assembly on Ageing, Vienna, July 26-Aug.6.

Desai, K.G., Bharat, & Veedon, R. (1993). Family dynamics and development programs. Indian course bibliography. *Indian Journal of Social Work, LIV*(1), 132-138.

Desai, K.G. & Naik, R.D. (1971). *Problems of retired people in Greater Bombay*, Tata Institute of Social Sciences, Bombay.

Gokhale, S.D. & Dave, C. (1992). *Services for elderly in India*. Paper circulated at International Federation on Ageing–First Global Conference, Bombay. Aug.-Sept.

Hypocrites Indians abuse the aged in a hundred ways. (1992). *Times of India*, Aug. 17, 13.

Jain & Menon. (1991). The greying of India, *India Today*, Sept. 30, 46-55.

Mehta, J. (1992). Sanyukta Chatta Vibhakta Kutumb. *Bombay Samachar Weekly*, Aug. 23, 13.

Mary, D.I. (N.D.). Violence committed by younger generation daughter and/or son-in-law on elder generation females. Unpublished paper.

Miranda, M.M. (1992). *Perspectives on the aged in India*. Unpublished paper presented at the National Workshop on "Developing curriculum for training volunteers." Tata Institute of Social Sciences, Bombay.

No one lets you age gracefully here. (1992). *Times of India*, Aug. 17.

Quinn, M.J. (1987). Elder abuse and neglect. In G.L. Maddox (ed.) *Encyclopedia on Aging*, New York: Springer Publishing Company, 203-204.

Ramamurthi, P.V. & Jamuna (1986). Self-other significant perceptions of issues and problems of middle aged and older women. Proceedings of XIth World Congress of Sociology of International Association of Sociology, New Delhi.

Ramamurthi, P.V. & Kullai, R.L. (1986). A study of the attitudes of different generations towards aging, *Psychological Studies, 31*(21), 126-130.

Vatuk, S. (1980). Withdrawing and disengagement as a cultural response to aging in India. In L.F. Christine (ed.) *Aging in culture and society*, New York: Bergin.

Venkoba Rao, A. (1985). Suicide In the Elderly. *Indian Journal of Social Psychiatry*, 3-10.

Chapter 8

Elder Abuse in the Republic of Ireland

Elizabeth Mary Horkan, MSocSc

INTRODUCTION

In view of the absence of officially recorded data regarding elder abuse, this exploratory chapter will outline the life situation of older people in Ireland, summarize available research material, overview social responses to the problem, and identify social policy issues which require attention.

Abuse of older people is one negative aspect of a remarkable twentieth century achievement that has improved quality of life and longevity for increasing proportions of the population. It is interesting to note that in a Eurobarometer survey, a higher percentage of Irish older people rated themselves as being treated with more respect (rather than less respect) as they grow older than do older people in other European Community countries (Commission of the European Communities 1992, p. 7). A recent study (O'Shea, 1993, p. 13) attributes Ireland's traditional relative inattention to the position of older age groups to its "bulging young population and the associated problems of unemployment and emigration." The data in Table 1 suggest why this may have been the case but also indicate why such inattention ought not to continue.

Elizabeth Mary Horkan is Lecturer, Department of Social Policy and Social Work, University College Dublin, Belfield, Ireland.

[Haworth co-indexing entry note]: "Elder Abuse in the Republic of Ireland." Horkan, Elizabeth Mary. Co-published simultaneously in the *Journal of Elder Abuse & Neglect* (The Haworth Press, Inc.) Vol. 6, No. 3/4, 1995, pp. 119-137; and: *Elder Abuse: International and Cross-Cultural Perspectives* (ed: Jordan I. Kosberg, and Juanita L. Garcia) The Haworth Press, Inc., 1995, pp. 119-137. Multiple copies of this article/chapter may be purchased from The Haworth Document Delivery Center [1-800-3-HAWORTH; 9:00 a.m. - 5:00 p.m. (EST)].

119

TABLE 1. Dependency Ratios.

Category	1961	1971	1981	1991	2001	2011	2021
60+ 20-59	0.35	0.35	0.32	0.31	0.29	0.34	0.44
<20 20-59	0.88	0.91	0.88	0.76	0.58	0.50	0.47

Sources: *Census of Population* (various years) and *Population and Labor Force Projections, 1991-2021 (CSO, 1988).* (O'Shea, 1993, p. 15).

DEMOGRAPHIC FEATURES
OF THE ELDERLY POPULATION

In 1991, the population of the Republic of Ireland was 3,523,401. The preliminary estimate of the elderly population, i.e., those over 65 years, was 394,830 (11.2%) of whom 56.8 percent were women. Five years earlier (the latest detailed figures available) those over 75 years numbered 143,861 of whom 60.5 percent were women. There were 25,458 people over 85, of whom 68.5 percent were women. Average life expectancy at birth is 71.0 years for males and 76.7 years for females (1985-7). These figures are among the lowest in the European Community.

Throughout this century, the fastest growth in the population has been in the oldest subgroups of the population over 65 years. Between 1986 and 2011, the elderly population as a whole is expected to increase by 14 percent. In the same period the 85 plus age group will increase by 55 percent. The increase in the oldest-old has implications for income maintenance because those over 75 have higher income needs, especially those living alone, and for health agencies because the older elderly are more vulnerable to illness and disability.

Women tend to live longer than men. In 1986, the number of women aged 85 years or older (17,449) was more than double the number of men in the same age group. Widows, who outnumber widowers by almost three to one among the elderly, account for 41 percent of women over 65. This percentage rises to 62 percent of those over 75 (Report to Government, 1993, p. 167).

Until now, the regions with the highest proportion of older people have been in the West of the country. It is estimated that this will change dramatically over the next 20 years with the decline in the Western region of 11-12 percent and an increase of 31 percent in the Eastern Health Board Region, which includes the greater Dublin area (Blackwell, 1985).

Two interesting aspects of Ireland's elderly population have been identified by Fogarty.

> The high fertility of the past means that for the coming decades the elderly in Ireland will have, compared to the rest of Europe, exceptionally large networks of adult descendants and the high proportion of the elderly never married. (EFILWC, 1987, p. 2-3)

For example, in 1960 the proportion never married at age 35-44 was 23 percent. Both these features have been changing in recent decades. In 1989, the birth rate showed a phenomenal decline to 14.7 from 21.9 in 1980. For the first time, Ireland's birth rate fell to below replacement level. By 1980 the proportion of population aged 35-44 never married had fallen to 11 percent, only a little above the proportions found in other European countries. It is, however, interesting to note that this had risen to 12.4 percent in 1988.

Living Arrangements

In 1986, 351,478 (91.5%) of all elderly people lived in private households in the community. Of this number, 81,174 (23.1%) lived alone, an 85 percent increase since 1971. The percentage living alone rises with age: 32,570 (26.2%) of those aged over 75 years lived alone and over 27 percent of women over 65 years were living alone in 1986.

Ireland has the highest rate (77%) of owner-occupied housing in the European Community (1981). Among the elderly, the rate is 80 percent; 67 percent of elderly householders own their home outright. Older people tend to live in the oldest housing stock, experiencing such problems as a lack of basic facilities (National Council for the Elderly, Factsheet No. 3, 1993).

Commenting on social exclusion in Ireland, a European Community Report estimates about 40 percent of elderly people live on their own or with their spouse only and many of them feel lonely and forgotten (Combatting Exclusion in Ireland, 1990-1994, 1993, p. 5). The isolation, loneliness, and need for social contact of the many elderly people living along has important implications for relatives and for voluntary and state agencies that care for the elderly. Among the elderly living alone, women outnumber men by 2 to 1 and the position of women tends to be financially much worse than men. Men tend to have less contact with statutory or voluntary agencies (NCA, 1989). As will be discussed later, older people living alone are also vulnerable to burglary and assault.

Incomes

Most elderly in Ireland receive either a non-contributory or contributory old age pension. The former is a means-tested social assistance payment, while the contributory pension is an entitlement under the national social insurance system. All employees in the country are covered directly or indirectly under the basic social insurance scheme. Currently, about half of the labor force are also covered under second tier occupational pensions, with numbers increasing steadily in recent years (Keogh & Whelan, 1985). However, women have less access to all kinds of resources through life, frequently not benefitting from a contributory pension (Report to Government, 1993). Although the older population has fared relatively well, and all the evidence points to a reduction in the risk of poverty for them as a group (Callan et al., 1989), the reality is that a small, but significant, number of elderly may be existing on very low incomes relative to their overall needs (O'Shea, 1993, p. 18-19).

VULNERABLE ELDERLY PEOPLE

An alarming statistic that could be interpreted as an indicator of institutionalized abuse or neglect is contained in the Green Paper on Mental Health 1992. It refers to over 3,000 long stay residential patients aged 65 years or over, few of whom have an active psychiatric component to their illness but who remain heavily institutionalized (p. 33). Other more widely recognized vulnerable groups include the older elderly (those aged 75 years and over), elderly living alone, pension dependent elderly households (i.e., those relying on state pensions for 70 percent or more of their income), and elderly women (NCA, 1989, p. 78).

While low income and poverty have been recognized as significant factors by NCA studies, vulnerability has tended to be defined other than as "at risk of abuse or violence." It is also recognized that:

> The vulnerability of elderly people may be caused or reinforced by factors other than inadequate income. These include homelessness, poor housing, inadequate means of access to essential services, inadequate screening for treatable illnesses, inadequate primary health and welfare services provision at the local level, inappropriate placement in institutional care, poor standards of institutional care provision, environmental hazards to the health, safety or security of elderly people, social behavior causing anxiety or fear, and inadequate social contact opportunities for the elderly living in the community or in institutions. (NCA, 1989, p. 79)

Elder support networks themselves tend to be fragile, often consisting of other elderly people (Horkan & Woods, 1986; Daly & O' Connor, 1984). It is interesting to note again that abuse is not explicitly mentioned.

Family Caring Network

A study undertaken for the National Council for the Aged in 1988 reported that three and a half times more old people are cared for at home by relatives than are cared for in institutions. It further states that this fact has major implications for the way future services will be planned, since an estimated 66,300 older persons receive a significant amount of care at home from family members. The carers are the persons who make it possible to carry out the policy objective. In spite of their critically important role, these carers go virtually unrecognized and unsupported by the state (NCA, 1989).

Referring to the above study, the Working Party on Services for The Elderly (1988) in their report *The Years Ahead–A Policy for the Elderly* (hereafter referred to as *The Years Ahead*) commented that the profile of carers suggests the need for a much greater recognition of the role of the family carer in policy and services for the elderly (p. 164). While insufficient support has been identified as a factor sometimes associated with violence by carers, it is important to recognize that carer stress is one of a number of dynamics associated with violence against old people. Society's perceptions of older people, psychological and psychiatric problems, substance abuse, social problems (such as inadequate housing, job loss or financial difficulties, unemployment) and factors within families, have all been linked to the phenomenon.

SOCIAL POLICY AND OLDER PEOPLE

As stated in the EFILWC report on Ireland (1987), three main policy guidelines had been proposed by the Darby Committee in their 1968 report on *The Care of the Aged*. The first declared that the aged are not a homogeneous group defined by chronological age or by any other single criterion such as poverty or disability. They are individuals with individual needs and potential, and policy towards them needs to be designed accordingly. The second said that it is better, and probably much cheaper, to help the elderly to live in the community with institutionalization as a last resort. The third recommended that services for the elderly be comprehensive, coordinated, and suitably adapted at local as well as national levels, across the voluntary as well as the statutory sectors (pp. 124-125).

In 1988, *The Years Ahead* (NCA, 1989) enunciated four objectives of public policy:

- to maintain elderly people in dignity and independence in their own home;
- to restore those elderly people who become ill or dependent to independence at home;
- to encourage and support the care of the elderly in their own community by family, neighbors, and voluntary bodies in every way possible; and

- to provide a high quality of hospital and residential care for elderly people when they can no longer be maintained in dignity and independence at home (p. 93).

Community Care

Ireland's community care package consists of three subprograms: (1) *community protection,* covering prevention of infectious diseases and health education, (2) *community health,* covering general practitioner services, drug supply, home nursing, dental, ophthalmic, and aural services, and (3) *community welfare* which includes personal social services, cash payments, and grants to voluntary welfare agencies. It has been observed that:

Ireland has always had a vibrant voluntary movement and its commitment to caring for elderly people, in particular, is unrivalled. This may be one of the reasons why the health boards have been slow to develop a professional social work involvement in the running of residential care and in support networks for keeping this client group in the community. Public health nurses and volunteers tend to dominate care for elderly people. (Fogarty M., EFILWC, 1987)

Coordination of Services

The Care of the Aged Interdepartmental Committee concluded in 1968 that "services are so varied and numerous that coordination at various levels is essential" (NCA, 1989, p. 110). Since that time the regional health boards established under the Health Act 1970 took over the administration of the health services from the local authorities, leaving the latter with the responsibility for housing.

The strategic significance of coordination derives from increased demand for support services at a time of budgetary restraint in a society characterized by erosion of the traditional family networks and increasing urbanization and youth emigration. These processes are exacerbated by decreased family size and fewer children to share what the NCA refers to as "the burden of care of elderly relatives." The growing participation of married women in the labor market is recognized as another factor that "reduces the number of informal unpaid care providers" (NCA, 1989, p. 111).

The NCA Report recommends a radically revised coordinated approach to the community care of elderly people based on an integrated continuum of comprehensive service for which a number of parties bear responsibility, including the family, the public, the medical and nursing professions, and the educational, housing, and health authorities. An interagency approach is to be adopted with an emphasis on collaboration and coordination to ensure the elimination of duplication and overlap in service provisions (NCA, 1989, p. 111).

VIOLENCE AGAINST OLDER PEOPLE

Vulnerability to Criminal Attack

Qualitative studies carried out in the 1980s identified safety and home security matters to be of concern and worry to elderly people living alone. Only two of the 45 people in one study (Horkan & Woods, 1986) felt it "quite safe for older people to live alone" and 30 of them believed that "it is never safe for an elderly person to do so." One-fifth of those involved in that study in suburban Dublin had been the victims of robbery and/or assault. Ironically, 30 respondents said that they themselves felt safe living alone.

The fact that the considerable security precautions many of them had taken to deter unwelcome intruders (i.e., locks, bolts, chains on doors, bars on windows, etc.) makes helpful intervention inaccessible. If an emergency occurred, an additional dilemma would confront elderly people (Horkan & Woods, 1986). A similar study conducted in a rural area (Daly & O'Connor, 1984) found "Home security or fear of being broken into and burgled is the greatest fear among elderly people in rural areas. It is not theft. per se, which worries them but the violence" (p. 94).

In December 1989, a television feature program entitled "Violence and the Elderly" portrayed seven older people who were described as victims of urban violence. Crimes committed against them included breaking and entering (5), robbery with violence (4), physical assault (4) and harassment (2). The four women and three men described being beaten up with assorted implements including a knuckleduster and a truncheon, one man had two arms broken, and one woman woke at night to find four men lying across her bed who threatened to kill her if she did not hand over the money. Some of them had quite large sums of money stolen. One woman described herself as surviving on medication for "environmental fear"; another described herself as a prisoner in her own home and asked the question "Who is the real prisoner? Is it me? or Is it the criminal who has imprisoned me?" (RTE, 19 December 1989).

In that program, Dr. Davis Coakley, Professor of Geriatric Medicine at Dublin's Trinity College, spoke of two problems for older people who experience attack. One of these is when the trauma followed by hospital admission is sometimes accompanied by an understandable reluctance to return to their home because it is no longer felt to be a safe haven. A second problem may arise when people who feel their homes are under threat of a break-in and who constantly refuse to go into a hospital for necessary treatment. Another TV Crimeline Feature program, called "Attack on the Elderly," featured a reconstructed attack in which imposters pretending to deliver free fuel, physically assaulted and robbed an elderly man in his own home. The purpose of this reconstruction was to serve as a warning to older people. The program advised "always check the identity of strangers before letting them in" (RTE, 1 February 1993).

In April 1993, the Minister of Health is reported to have "condemned attacks on the elderly and on children as the grossest forms of violence that society [has] witnessed." Within two days, three separate attacks all involving physical assault and theft (the sums of money were £10, £700, and £4,000) of the life-savings of an elderly brother and sister were reported (*Irish Independent*, April 23,1993).

Vulnerability to Domestic Abuse

Definitions. The suggested working definition of abuse employed by the Council of Europe Study (1992), "A non-accidental act or omission which undermines the life, the physical or psychological integrity of an older person or that seriously harms the development of his or her personality and/or undermines or damages his or her financial security," is utilized in the pages that follow. The types and manifestations of abuse are:

Physical: hitting, beating, pushing, sticking fingers in eyes, shaking, inappropriate touching and sexual abuse.

Psychological: verbal, threatening, isolation, moral blackmail.

Financial: fraud, possession of money and valuables, refusal to pay bills, cashing pension on the older person's behalf, retention of a share of pension, appropriation of trinkets, cash.

Denial of rights: isolation in separate building or in remote part of shared dwelling, refusal to admit visitors.

Although the accepted age for retirement is 65 years, increasing numbers of workers retire before this age. Thus, "age of retirement" may be utilized to represent the older population.

A pioneering case study article by Coakley (1990) details three examples of abuse against elderly women by their daughters. It is significant that these three cases were admitted to one Dublin hospital within one month. In a special issue of the *Irish Social Worker* in Summer 1990 entitled "Focus on Old Age," a discursive article on "Abuse of Older People in the Domestic Setting" by Ann O'Loughlin, a social worker, included illustrative cases and comment. This provoked media interest and resulted in newspaper and radio news coverage and some magazine articles.

In February 1991, the writer, then a Council of Europe Fellowship holder, addressed an International Conference in Trinity College Dublin on Elder Abuse. The press coverage of which, despite a balanced reporting of content, received the unfortunately sensational headline "Old Folk Bullied, Beaten in Homes" (*E. Herald*, 9th February, 1991). That same year, O'Loughlin compiled a report entitled "Awaiting Advocacy–Elder Abuse and Neglect in Ireland" as part of a post-qualifying course at the University of Southampton. The report cited 13 cases that covered a wide range of abuse: physical, psychological, sexual, financial, deprivation of rights and excessive use of medication. Some cases included more than one kind of abuse. The relationships of the abuser to the abused included spouse (male and female), son, daughter, daughter-in-law, and nephew. In some cases, several family members were implicated.

Excerpts from that study have been reported recently under the title "The Hidden Scandal: Abuse of the Elderly." The article contrasts the major social policy initiatives that have been taken regarding child abuse and wife beating with the lack of procedures to deal with elder abuse. O'Loughlin expresses the hope that similar developments will occur "without having to wait for scandals such as happened in child abuse" (*Irish Times*, 13th April 1993, p. 10). According to the accumulated evidence, scandalous incidents would seem to have occurred already.

Legal Responses to Elder Abuse

The basis of the Irish Code of Law is still the Common Law of England. There is no specific legislation concerning family violence and elderly people. The Irish Criminal Law provides protection for all citizens against violence, and there are many offenses with which people who abuse others can be charged. The only age-related legislation is Protective Legislation concerning young people.

A victim of domestic violence may apply for an injunction, which is essentially an order of the court directing a person to do or to refrain from doing a particular act and to exclude the perpetrator from the family home. A spouse may apply for a barring order under the Family Law (Protection of Spouses and Children) Act 1981. The latter is cheaper, the procedure is simpler, and there are criminal remedies for breach of its orders. The grounds for either of the above options is that the court "should be satisfied that there are reasonable grounds for believing that the safety or welfare of (the applicant) spouse or any dependent children of the family requires it" (Shatter, 1987, p. 590).

It is a common law misdemeanor to refuse or neglect to provide sufficient food or other necessities to life to any person such as a child or aged or sick person unable to, under certain conditions, take care of himself/herself. Reported difficulties in using legal proceedings, in particular criminal charges to protect older people, include difficulties in sustaining allegations because it is easy for an old person's assertions to be attributed to forgetfulness or paranoia, pressing charges because of the reluctance of elderly people out of embarrassment or guilt or "family pride"; and obtaining corroborative evidence from third parties.

Allegations about the reluctance of the Irish police to become involved in domestic violence incidents is strongly challenged by the results of a survey involving 300 such incidents in April-June 1992. The author of this survey concluded that the police primarily see themselves in a counselling role with regard to domestic violence as opposed to a strictly policing function. Also, the police believed that many incidents of such violence are most appropriately dealt with in the civil law (Morgan, 1992).

It is important that legal measures be framed in such a way as to avoid infringing on the right to self-determination and the right to refuse medical treatment, but which accommodate the concept of 'acceptable risk.' Wrigley (1990), a psychogeriatrician, has drawn attention to the disadvantages pertaining to existing options for elderly people when protective intervention is necessary and suggests alternatives. She has also identified the lack of a mechanism to protect those being abused by their relatives and the difficulty in providing care for those at-risk through self neglect other than in a psychiatric setting. She suggests that guardianship measures would ensure their protection. Statutory provision is required to safeguard the elderly being abused by pathological carers similar to that used in child abuse cases.

Enduring Power of Attorney (not presently available in Ireland) would ensure the wishes of older persons were recognized in managing their financial affairs. This is particularly appropriate when relatives are involved, and *Ward of Court Order* would remain a satisfactory method for dementing people without relatives. However, disadvantages of Wardship include lengthy proceedings and the requirement that elderly persons be defined as mentally incapable of managing their affairs (which is often not the case). At present, protective intervention under the Mental Treatment Acts 1945-1961 requires that a person be admitted to a Psychiatric Unit. This action can lead to their inappropriate association with very disturbed psychiatric patients (Wrigley, 1990).

In March 1991, Dr. Wrigley again highlighted the problem of abused elderly people and drew attention to a "small group" of "pathological carers" who abuse not because of stress from the burden of caring but more for reasons of gain or gratification" (Wrigley, 1991). She contrasts two kinds of abusing relative: one group are 'stressed carers,' those burdened by a complex mix of internal and external stresses who become exhausted and abuse as a consequence, who should not be condemned but helped sensitively. The less common 'pathological carers' include those who have learned to use violence as an integral part of family life-style and as a means of communication, and/or those whose individual problems are the sole determinants of family violence. Examples include drug and alcohol abuse, sociopathic behavior, mental retardation, and psychiatric disorders (Wrigley, 1991).

The proposals in the Green Paper seek to remedy defects in the current provision and aim to provide a legal means of protecting those who are not receiving proper care and attention in the least restrictive manner possible. The paper declared: "It is not proposed in new legislation to allow for their detention in a psychiatric center," is welcomed (Green Paper on Mental Health, 1992, p. 105). There is also a commitment to seek improvements regarding Supervision Orders and the views of members of the public are being sought in this regard.

Social Policy Recognition of Elder Abuse

A perennial question confronting social policy analysts is: Does recognition of and concern about social policy issues emerge as a result of a real increase in the incidence of phenomena in society or are these a function of improved levels of awareness and understanding among social policy and social service personnel? No official statistics are published regarding violence against older people from court, police, or hospital records. Criminal statistics, published annually, give the age of criminals but not that of victims.

It is interesting to note that in April 1991 the Minister for Health was asked a parliamentary question concerning the number of reported cases of abuse of the elderly. He was requested to take steps to introduce guidelines concerning improved recognition and to establish a formal procedure involving care teams and community directors. The Minister for Health responded that "no cases of abuse of the elderly were formally reported to me in 1989 or 1990." He continued "The Health Boards maintain registers of "Elderly at-Risk" and their professional staff are alert for possible abuse of the elderly. I am satisfied that these health care personnel are competent to recognize any case of abuse and deal with them as necessary. In the circumstances I have no plans at present to introduce a formal reporting procedure but I am prepared to reconsider the matter should the necessity arise" (Dail Questions, April, 1989).

Recognition of Abuse

Having acknowledged that "insufficient support is available to thousands of relatives caring for the elderly at home, many of whom have severe disabilities" (WPSE, 1988, p. 24), *The Years Ahead* included the first official recognition of the possibility of elder abuse. "In a small number of cases, intense strain on the carer *can* result in the physical and emotional abuse of elderly people" and the report concedes "The need of dependent elderly people and their carers for a service to help these problems has not been officially recognized up to now (p. 98)." The report anticipates "greater attention will need to be given to resolving interpersonal problems" (p. 98) and recommends "that a domiciliary counselling service be available to elderly people and their families and that the community care social work departments be gradually expanded for this purpose" (p. 99). It allocates case finding of at-risk elderly people to the General Medical Service, (p. 84) and states the "District Nurse should be aware of all elderly people receiving a significant amount of care from their families or neighbors" (p. 83).

In January 1993, a government appointed commission referring to older women, stated "They are more vulnerable to isolation, loneliness, and even bullying than older men" (pp. 167-8) and continued "In some cases the elderly may be left in the care of adult children who do not want them and where stress and other factors such as alcohol could precipitate elder abuse" (Report to Government, January, 1993, p. 168).

These two recent acknowledgements of elder abuse tend to attribute it to carer stress. In Ireland, popular perceptions tend to identify the source of violence against old people as coming from outside the family and to assume that older people within the family setting are receiving at least adequate support and care. It is a matter of some concern that a recent upsurge in the incidence of family tension and stress, sometimes resulting in elder abuse, was reported to the writer by representatives of three voluntary organizations in 1993. One helpline for women cited 12 cases in the past year involving older women. In almost all cases the abuser was the spouse. A second agency working with families confirmed the existence of elder abuse, identified husbands as the usual abuser and violence as "usually a long-standing feature of the marriage." Another helpline involved with stressed parents recognized an emerging pattern of middle-aged and older parents, whose adult children continue to live with them, complaining of both verbal and physical violence. Regarding the increase in family violence, these three agencies link the phenomenon to the increase in the number of unemployed young and sometimes middle-aged adults who, lacking resources for independent living, consequently remain in or return to the family home. In Ireland, the overall level of unemployment is extremely high at 302,000 or 21 percent of the labor force (January 1993) (E.C. Report, 1992/1993).

EMPOWERMENT OF OLDER PEOPLE

Social Participation and Empowerment of Older People

There has been a tendency to see the needs of older people within a framework and philosophy dominated by health and social care issues. Fogarty's 1987 study commented that ". . . one feature missing in Ireland is an age lobby as well organized and forceful as those which are found in countries like The Netherlands." Only in recent years has attention been paid to aspects of social integration and participation in a wide range of activities and institutions.

In October 1988, the Irish Congress of Trade Unions and the National Federation of Pensioners Associations jointly issued a "Charter of Rights for the Elderly," which includes the right to protection against violence and the right to participate in and be represented on appropriate bodies dealing with matters concerning the elderly. A year and one-half later, the Irish Association of Older People (of which the writer is a Director) was incorporated as a limited company. Its objectives include "to serve as the direct voice for older people and, based on the principle of self-help, to achieve recognition of the value and capacity of older people."

The Association works cooperatively with other organizations of elderly people. It proposes to establish a telephone helpline for older people. In recent years, a country-wide Age and Opportunity Movement is helping to create and project positive images of growing old in Ireland. The processes are being reinforced by varied activities scheduled for 1993 European Year of Older People and of solidarity between generations. These developments suggest the emergence of an articulate socially concerned elderly lobby in Ireland.

Community Support Services Against Violence

In addition to community care services already outlined, Community Alert, a country-wide crime prevention movement based on neighborly cooperation, exists for the protection of rural communities, especially vulnerable elderly people, in cooperation with the police. This movement began in response to a number of attacks on elderly people, in 1984 and 1985, who were then being targeted for criminal attack and robbery by a gang. The movement continues to operate effectively. Neighborhood Watch, a scheme operating in urban areas, includes concern for vulnerable elderly people as part of its brief. The Irish Association for Victim Support receives over 2,000 calls annually. It is regrettable that no statistical analysis of the age range of callers is available. Other voluntary agencies like those already mentioned operate in a supportive capacity.

The General Medical Practitioner is identified by many as the person most likely to be consulted in relation to domestic violence. Within both the Irish Nurses Organization and the Irish Association of Social Workers, there are special interest groups that concern themselves with the needs of older people. The Carers Association provides psychological and social support and has responded to about 1000 calls or inquiries since its foundation in the mid-80s. As stated earlier, there is a tendency to resort to the protective use of residential care, a process that removes victims from their home surroundings. Whether or not this is in their best interest is a matter of some conjecture. Respite care facilities are used quite extensively to relieve stressed carers.

Prevention

There are no special preventive programs regarding family violence and older people. A wide range of community-based services and structures can be used in a supportive, protective or preventive way. The self-help movements, already discussed, are likely to make contributions to the welfare of elderly people by helping them to be more pro-active and self-assertive.

CONCLUSION

Despite the recent emergence of a number of articles on the topic, it would be an exaggeration to state the problem of elder abuse has received official recognition in Ireland. However, there are hopeful signs that relevant issues are being addressed with a degree of seriousness by concerned parties. A key question is whether elder abuse should be addressed as a separate issue within other social policy developments. The philosophies and energies of the Women's Movement together with the recent dramatic escalation in the recognition of domestic violence (a discussion of which is beyond the scope of this chapter), as issues requiring intervention by doctors and police, suggest that elder abuse may best be responded to within these developments. An interesting initiative was the announcement in April 1993 of a police plan to focus on crime against women, with a five-year corporate strategy that gives top priority to violence against women, juvenile crime, and law-breaking in disadvantaged urban areas, followed by support for elderly people living alone (*Irish Times*, 9/10 April, 1993).

That elder abuse is not only a social care and social welfare issue but also a socio-cultural and political one is indisputable. Responses need to be framed accordingly and to address the issues of civil rights and social justice.

REFERENCES

Blackwell J. (1985). Appendix 2: *Population projections by county and planning region 1981-2006 in housing for the elderly in Ireland*, National Council for the Aged, Dublin.

Callan, T., Hannan, D., Nolan, B., Whelan, B.J. & Creighton, S. (1989). *The measurement of poverty and social welfare effectiveness in Ireland.*

Carey, S. & Carroll, B. (1986). *Patchwork–Establishing the needs of the elderly at the local level.*

Census of Population, 1986.

Coakley, D. et al. (1990). Elder abuse, *Irish Journal of Medical Science, 159*(2), 48-49.

Council of Europe, 1992. *Violence against elderly people.*

Department of Health, 1992. Green Paper on Mental Health.

Dully, C., & Rooney, H. (1992). *Alone in later life, Athlone Community Services Council.*

Eastern Health Board. (1989). *Services for the elderly.*

European Commission. (1993). *Combatting exclusion in Ireland, 1990-1994*, A Midway Report.

European Foundation for the Improvement of Living and Working Conditions. (1987). *Social conditions and time available for assistance to the elderly–Report on Ireland*, (Fogarty, M.P.).

Horkan M. & Woods A. (1986). *This is our world: Perspectives of some elderly people on life in Suburban Dublin.*

Interdepartmental Committee on the Care of the Aged. (1968). *(The Darby Report) The care of the aged.*

Keogh, G., & Whelan, B. (1985). *Survey of employer pension schemes: Report to the Department of Social Welfare*, Dublin, The Economic and Social Research Institute.

Morgan, M. (1992) *Gardai and domestic violence incidents: A Profile based on a national sample of investigations.* Paper presented to the Conference on Safety for Women, October 3rd.

NCA. (1989). *Report on its second term of office.*

NCA. (1984). *Incomes of the elderly in Ireland.*

NCA. (1985). *Housing for the elderly in Ireland.*

National Council for the Elderly (NCE). (1993). Factsheet No. 3. *Ageing in Ireland basic facts.*

O'Connor, J. & Daly M (1984). *The world of the elderly: The rural experience.*

O'Connor, J. et al. (1988). *Caring for the elderly: Part I: A study of carers at home and in the community*, NCA.

O'Connor, J. et al, (1988). *Caring for the elderly: Part II: A study of carers in the home.*

O'Loughlin, A. (1990). *Old age abuse in the domestic setting*, Irish Soc. Worker, pp. 4-7.

O'Loughlin, A. (1991). *Awaiting advocacy–Elder abuse and neglect in Ireland*, Unpublished Report Presented to University of Southampton.

O'Shea, E. (1993). *The impact of social and economic policies on older people in Ireland*, NCE Report No. 24.

Power, B. (1980). *Old and alone in Ireland.*

Second Report of the Commission on the Status of Women. (1993). *Report to Government–January 1993.*

Shatter, Alan. (1987). *Family law in the Republic of Ireland.*

South Inner City Community Development Association. (1986). *A community study of the needs of the elderly in Dublin's liberties.*

Working Party on Services for The Elderly. (1988). *The years ahead: A policy for the elderly.*

Wrigley, M. (1990) New measures needed to safeguard the elderly, *Irish Medical News*, 7(5), 9.

Wrigley, M. (1991). Abuse of elderly people–Pathological carers, *Irish Medical Journal, 81*, March.

Chapter 9

Norway:
Weakness in Welfare

Sigurd Johns, MA
Ida Hydle, MD, PhD

Norway is a small country in the north of Europe, consisting of 4 million people. Like the rest of Scandinavia, it is a rather affluent industrialized nation with a long tradition of social democracy. The well-reputed organization of health and social services (called "the welfare state") means, basically, that a comprehensive health and social security scheme covers the whole population. Norwegians themselves have a firm belief in the welfare state, and there has been little worry about growing old.

With the current economic decline and resulting cuts in budgets, the attitude has changed. Given the relative growth in the old population, the ability to manage the cost of pension schemes and health care for the elderly is questioned. The discovery of elder abuse in Norway and the resulting development of measures must be understood in this context. A recent report by the Norwegian Ministry of Social Affairs, "Safety-Dignity-Care" (NOU 1, 1992), underlines

Sigurd Johns is Social Anthropologist, University Department of Medicine, Ullevaal Hospital, 0407 Oslo 4, Norway. Ida Hydle is Project Coordinator, Ministry of Social Affairs and Director, European and Nordic Studies on Family Violence Against the Elderly.

[Haworth co-indexing entry note]: "Norway: Weakness in Welfare." Johns, Sigurd, and Ida Hydle. Co-published simultaneously in the *Journal of Elder Abuse & Neglect* (The Haworth Press, Inc.) Vol. 6, No. 3/4, 1995, pp. 139-156; and: *Elder Abuse: International and Cross-Cultural Perspectives* (ed: Jordan I. Kosberg, and Juanita L. Garcia) The Haworth Press, Inc., 1995, pp. 139-156. Multiple copies of this article/chapter may be purchased from The Haworth Document Delivery Center [1-800-3-HAWORTH; 9:00 a.m. - 5:00 p.m. (EST)].

139

the rights of the elderly to sufficient quality of life and fulfillment of caring needs. There is a concern about the increasing costs of care. This chapter discusses the problems now developing, how to cope with them, and possible reforms. Elder abuse in the family is recognized as a 'new' problem demanding special attention.

Still, the public debate recommending transferring care for the elderly from institutions to the home and family has not made working with elder abuse easier. More and more concern is voiced (heard) about the so-called "wave of the elderly" as if Norwegians are facing some kind of natural disaster. (For a critical discussion of the "misery perspective," see Tornstam, 1992.)

A GENERAL OVERVIEW OF THE ELDERLY IN NORWAY

Old, Single, Female, and Living at Home

In a worldwide perspective, the elderly in Norway can be described as relatively healthy and wealthy. They work until the age of 67, they grow old, many are active members of society; they receive free health and social services, and everyone is covered by a pension-scheme. But there are big differences among groups of elderly in living conditions and health. (The population is quite homogeneous in terms of religion, culture, and ethnicity. The information in this chapter derives from the Protestant Nordic majority, mostly represented by middle- and working-class city-dwellers of Oslo.)

In 1990, the retired (67 and older) represented 14 percent of the total population. The proportion of elderly who are above 80 years has more than tripled in the last 50 years. As in most other countries, Norwegian women live longer than men. Calculated life expectancy of the 65-year old female is 83, and 79 for males (Norwegian Statistics, 1988). For the group above 80 years, two-thirds are women (164,000 in total) and most of them live alone. From 1960 to 1980, the increase in elderly over 80 (living alone at home) was from 24 to 57 percent. Single older women living at home are predominantly an urban phenomenon. The urban population comprises 60 percent of the total Norwegian population. Future projections regarding the population over 80 indicate that, in 2015, 90 percent will be living alone (Helset, 1991). Single elderly persons consume more than twice the caring services received by those living with somebody. Thus, the growth of a large old-old, female population (with greater vulnerability) is a challenge to planning caring services. Concerning elder abuse, it is important to note that the old, single, physically and/or mentally impaired widow is in a high-risk position. This situation is no less so, even if she has money, although wealth might reduce some of the negative consequences of financial abuse.

There has been a tendency to institutionalize elderly people in Norway. Some years ago, there were more nursing home beds than hospital beds. Partly as a result of rising nursing home bed costs, partly due to municipal needs for saving money, and partly due to a shift in ideology, elderly people needing care are now maintained in their homes for as long as possible. Home care is provided partly by close kin, especially spouses and daughters, but also by professionals. Locally-organized home care by nurses and home-helpers is a major resource in the health care for the elderly.

In 1988, there were 17,000 residents in homes for the elderly (social institutions), while 30,000 were permanent residents in nursing homes (medical institutions). An important group of the elderly being cared for within institutions are patients with organic brain diseases (or other diseases resulting in dementia). There are about 50,000 individuals with such disorders in Norway who need specialized care (ranging from proper diagnostic management to sheltered homes to sheltered wards in nursing homes). Many of them are dependent upon the care from their close kin, and thus constitute a distinct high-risk group for abuse and neglect.

Modernization of society has resulted in diminishing the importance of the family in most people's life. Family relations are growing more complex and unstable, with geographic mobility, divorce, remarriage, and personal independence within cohabitant couples. A high rate of women (70 percent) is engaged in wage-work outside the home; children have a looser, more autonomous relation to their parents; and caring obligations are unclear compared to the past. On the one hand, both small children and the elderly are cared for by professionals; on the other, many healthy pensioners are crucial in the care of their grandchildren during working hours.

It is probable that the "opening up" of society and the family is one of the reasons why awareness of all kinds of family violence has increased. Paradoxically, however, within this "looser" society, the privacy of the home may become more closed and restricted than ever before so that family violence exists in secrecy and seclusion.

ELDER ABUSE

Discovering the Problem

Elder abuse was "discovered" in Norway as a result of reports and articles from the U.S. in the beginning of the 1980s. Because of the belief in the effective functioning of the welfare state, Norwegian researchers, health-care administrators, and policymakers ignored the problem. Several individuals categorically refused to believe that elder abuse existed in Norway. The lack of awareness of the problem was alarming.

But the discovery was not "news" to everybody. Professionals within health care and social services had been struggling with the problem, but using the term "elder abuse" had not occurred to them. The pioneers in the field, by naming the problem, were able to organize the most difficult cases drawn from scattered experience into an explicit category. In 1983, Grete Stang and Åsa Rytter Evensen (1985) conducted the first survey among home nurses in Oslo and found that 1 percent of the patients suffered abuse by a family member in one form or another. Following the presentation of these results (exposed in the media), the Ministry of Social Affairs undertook the task of increasing knowledge and developing measures of the problem.

Ida Hydle, who has worked with Stang since 1983, assisted in authoring the first Norwegian handbook for professionals (Stang & Hydle, 1986). The two made a Ministry sponsored visit to the U.S. and incorporated what they learned in the handbook. Hydle, who at the time was working as a physician in a geriatric ward, had gained practical experience with elderly victims of abuse. It seemed to her that the American findings on abuse were also highly relevant in Norway. Although more knowledge was needed about the effect of the difference in the Norwegian population and in the organization of society on the problem, no longer was there any doubt that there were Norwegian victims of elder abuse.

Planning more extensive research, Hydle decided to focus on the nature of elder abuse rather than the extent of the problem: firstly, because epidemiological studies would be difficult to design, as elder abuse is hard to define and often remains concealed in the privacy of home and family, and secondly, because priority should be given to learning how to help the victims since special measures, competence and knowledge were virtually nonexistent.

In 1988, the Ministry granted funding for a research project to the authors of this chapter, a medical doctor and a social anthropologist. Employing an interdisciplinary approach, they focused on an extensive, in-depth analysis of individual cases of abuse. Material was based on referrals to the University Department of Geriatric Medicine of Ullevaal Hospital in Oslo. Taking for granted the existence of the problem, the study concentrated on the problem and how to help the abused. It was reasonable to believe that other researchers working in other countries could gain from using a similar approach. The same kind of research-strategy was applied in a Pan-European study, as noted in the report: "Recognizing the virtual impossibility of attempting to establish the extent of violence against elderly people, the Study Group decided to examine the extent of knowledge, understanding and awareness" (Council of Europe, 1992, p. 13).

Based on study results, Hydle and Johns were able to develop a version of the U.S. "Adult Protective Services" system designed to comply with Norwegian culture and social policy. With the establishment of this kind of service, cases of elder abuse are identified and reports received (thus supplying data useful for study and analysis). Giving priority to developing measures to avoid identifying problems that society cannot handle properly is an obvious ethical dilemma. Though still lacking reliable scientific results, the authors estimated that 3 to 5 percent of the elderly living at home are victims of abuse in a general sense of the term (self-neglect not included, see below).

Key Problem Number 1: The Definition of Elder Abuse

In defining elder abuse, practitioners and researchers in Europe and the United States have included everything from physical violence and rape, at one extreme, to infantilization, inadequate care, and lack of respect, at the other. Acts of economic exploitation and material abuse are often included, as well (Pillemer & Wolf, 1986; Kosberg & Cairl, 1986; Hugonot, 1990; Council of Europe, 1992; Decalmer & Glendenning, 1993). A definite lack of focus complicates estimating the extent of the problem, developing interventions, and analyzing elder abuse as a single problem. The insecurity of the practitioners (having to decide whether and how to intervene) is not eased by these all-embracing definitions. A basic problem is that abuse is a subject loaded with emotions. What may seem abusive to one person may not seem so to another.

The Council of Europe study group, in which the authors of this chapter participated, discussed and rejected all existing definitions. Recognizing the three dimensions of family violence against elderly people, the group adopted the following solution: First, *family* was defined to include: "... anyone related to him or her by blood, marriage, or cohabitation." Second, *violence* was specified as: "... any act or omission . . ." that may somehow be harmful (bodily, psychologically or financially). Third, *elderly people* were stated to be: "... persons at or above national retirement ages ..." (Council of Europe, 1992, p. 21).

These extrinsic definitions described the object of study and served the purpose of guiding an investigation into the knowledge and experience of officials and professionals. The advantage of the definition for analytical purposes and the reason for referring to it here is the very explicit recognition of three interrelated dimensions. Further, as made clear in the reference to national retirement ages, the study group recognized national and cultural variation in the understanding of the terms. As for violence, the group stated that "... in the last analysis, definition and diagnosis depend on the subjective value judgment of each researcher and practitioner involved" (Council of Europe, 1992, p. 18).

In the American literature, an amazing amount of effort has been spent in elaborating on definitions of abuse, while the meaning of age and family has seemingly been taken for granted. To illustrate, both Tanya Johnson (1986) and Margaret Hudson (1991) were concerned about the lack of comprehensive definitions of elder abuse, made their own attempts at identifying problems (by different approaches) and came up with more universal definitions. Still, both authors seemed to take the meaning of family as self-evident. When it comes to age, the two authors recognized the problem, but avoided going into it or proposing a satisfying definition. Hudson briefly referred to the link between old age and frailty (1991, p. 8), but mentioned no age limit. In an earlier article, she reported that 60 was the age limit used in most research (1986, p. 128). Johnson stated that "[chronological] age itself is not really an adequate indication of being old" (1986, p. 183). She discussed the implications of this, and even considered the possibility of abandoning age as a criterion altogether. She finally proposed 70 as an age limit, arguing that this was in keeping with the arbitrariness of the age of retirement.

Norway, too, has been using retirement age as an initial limit. The reasons are mainly political. However, after experience with an ever-increasing variety of cases, the authors have been forced to ask some difficult questions. For instance: What about the 55 year-old single mother being brutalized by her son? She has the same problem as mothers 20 years older. What about the 80 year-old wife who has been severely mistreated by her husband for 50 years? Why distinguish between wife-battering and elder abuse in her case? What about the frail and demented old man being abused and neglected by his close kin? Is not his disease (sickness) a more relevant factor than his chronological age (date of birth)?

The above is not to say that age has nothing to do with it, but to call for a critical discussion of the "elder" in "elder abuse." In a (Norwegian) textbook (Hydle & Johns, 1992), the authors have elaborated on six different aspects of aging: Chronological age, social celebration of aging (the rites of passage), the subjective experience of aging, the physiological process of irreversible bodily changes, the mental processes of aging, and aging as an element in personal identity. "Social aging," which depends on (gender) sex, family status, health, class, culture, and several other factors, is subject to much manipulation and negotiation on the part of the individual. It can be seen as a sum total of all the other aspects of aging and is simultaneously the most difficult and the most important to grasp through definitions.

Abuse and Morality

In the literature on family violence, various attempts have been made to unify definitions. The focus has been on harm and injuries or various conceivable acts and omissions associated with treatment of elderly people. This kind of definition is what Hudson and Johnson term "extrinsic." The search for a "valid intrinsic definition" is the main topic of both Hudson and Johnson's work. As Johnson (1986, p. 169) states: "Intrinsic definitions are conspicuously absent from the elder mistreatment literature." The Norwegian authors prefer using the terms "descriptive" (extrinsic) and "analytical" (intrinsic) when discussing the matter.

Johnson has chosen the obvious strategy, targeting the linguistic meaning of the construct. She proposes the following analytical definition of abuse: "self- or other-inflicted suffering unnecessary to the maintenance of the quality of life of the older person" (1986, p. 180). She is taking into account that not all suffering can be or should be avoided. But, since "unnecessary" becomes a key term, she ends up with the problem from which she needs to escape. What criteria do we have to differentiate between unnecessary and necessary suffering? Johnson proposes to clarify the term "abuse" but ends up with the equally vague and value-laden term "unnecessary." This puzzle has a tendency to occur in most definitions of abuse.

Hudson (1991, p. 2) has likewise recognized the basic problem: "Further, the meanings of the concepts are culturally determined, value-laden, and emotionally charged, and have ethical ramifications. Thus, agreement on definitions is difficult and sometimes even inappropriate." From this very promising outset, she ends up relying on inaccurate terms and categories like "unnecessary suffering," "adequate and reasonable assistance," "basic needs," and "harmful effects" (Hudson, 1991, p. 14).

To avoid this puzzle, one must confront the very basic implication of value-judgment in terms like abuse. Bluntly stated, the difference between treatment and mistreatment is the prefix "mis."

Any attempt at construing a satisfying analytical definition of abuse must specify the social and moral nature of the problem. An act of abuse is, as we have argued elsewhere, "A two-headed monster of injury *and offense*" (Johns et al., 1991). Starting out with an approach similar to Johnson and Hudson, Johns et al. (1991) questioned the meaning of the concept, particularly the content of value. Relying on the interpretive capacity of semiology and social anthropology, the authors were able to take the analysis a step further. Semiology, the science of meaning, offers some basic analytical tools. Applying these tools makes it possible to separate the *form* of the (possible) abusive act from the *content*, the meaning, and value, of the act. Causing suffering is not necessarily wrong; even health professionals may do it to treat patients. The wrongness of the act, the content of abuse, depends on situational and culture-specific value judgments. It is necessary to include this aspect when formulating a definition (Johns et al., 1991).

In discussing the dynamics of violence, anthropologist David Riches (1986) has presented a solution. He sees violence as a two-level power struggle. At the primary level, violence signifies a struggle between contenders. At the secondary level, both parties (and certainly the stronger party) will try to convince others that the right is on his or her side. Riches, thus, identifies the basic *triangle of violence* which involves not only victim and perpetrator but also others (directly or indirectly) witnessing the act. By including the generalized "witness" in a definition, "the value-puzzle" can be solved. A basic lesson from Riches is that when terms like abuse or violence are being used, ". . . attention should crucially be focused on *who* is labeling a given act as such, and most especially their social position" (1986, p. 4).

From this beginning, the following analytical definition was developed (Johns et al., 1991, Hydle & Johns, 1992):

> Abuse is a social act involving at least two actors, one of whom is violating the personal boundaries of the other. This is abuse insofar as it is interpreted and morally evaluated as illegitimate by a third party, the witness.

This definition has been utilized in research, education, and practice in Norway. It is not simple and objective, but neither is the topic. It has several advantages. In research, it directs attention towards who is labeling an act as abuse (and why). In education, it serves as a basis for preparing the student for the professional dilemmas related to becoming a "witness" (Saveman et al., 1993). Further, in education and practice, it has the advantage of making the ethics involved explicit, rather than concealing ethics behind more or less objective criteria. Diagnosing and identifying abuse implies a judgment of other people's behavior. By using the expression "violating personal boundaries," the attempt has been made to capture the very essential victim's experience of deprivation and intrusion and link it to central concepts of therapeutic treatment (Johns et al., 1991). This approach is important in education and practice. Although the expression serves the purpose of the analytical definition, its brevity clearly calls for the corollary of descriptive definitions.

Cultural Difference, What Is Specific to Norway?

Using the term violation in the definition implies acts rather than omissions although this in not the intention. Possible misunderstandings can be prevented by reference to descriptive definitions. Since it is the intention to involve two actors, self-neglect is ruled out even though it is a major type of abuse in the U.S. As was suggested elsewhere (Johns et al., 1992), the question of self-neglect is a clue to the difference in ideologies of health care between U.S. and Norway. The problem of poverty is small in Norway but does exist. Similarly, although alcoholism, drug abuse, and psychiatric disorder (or eccentric ideas leading to extreme uncleanliness or other high-risk behavior) do exist among the Norwegian elderly, these cases are not classified under the heading of self-neglect. In the ideology of comprehensive welfare and solidarity between citizens, the authorities are responsible for the well-being of the elderly. Consequently, if an old person should be found living in unacceptable conditions, the local health administration is more liable to be accused of neglect than the old person. The difference, thus, is related more to culture and organization of society than to the occurrence of problems. Cross-cultural discussion about this kind of difference is important. Learning about the concept of self-neglect in the U.S. has increased awareness in Norway. Choosing to rule it out is not simply a matter of right or wrong, but rather a matter of considering cultural and societal values.

Comparing Norway to Great Britain, another pioneer country in the field of elder abuse, identifies another apparent difference. British policymakers and researchers have concentrated on mistreatment of dependent and vulnerable elderly by carers (Eastman, 1984; Bennett, 1990; Pritchard, 1992; Decalmer & Glendenning, 1993). The caring relation between frail elderly and their close kin seems to be a primary focus, to the extent that the geriatrician Gerry Bennett has suggested redefining elder abuse in terms of "inadequate care" (Bennett, 1990). [Note: Bennett actually prefers adopting the term from U.S. researchers, Fulmer and O'Malley (1987)].

However, in Norway, the focus is on conflict rather than quality of care. Illness and strained caring relations are regarded as two of several possible sources of conflict. (It is interesting, though slightly speculative, to interpret the preoccupation with family conflict in the light of central Norwegian values. The anthropologist Marianne Gullestad (1991) has identified home, privacy, and "peace and quiet" as indications of the good life, and consequently family conflicts should be regarded as a most serious problem by Norwegians.)

More variations can be found but one should not look for cultural differences primarily in the extent and occurrence of cases. Although comparisons along those dimensions are relevant, the most important differences are found in the conceptions of what constitutes elder abuse. Notably, conceptions of abuse also influence calculations of extent and theories about causation. Cultural comparison is facilitated by the kind of analytical definition used. It would be of great interest to further explore cultural differences. Two main topics in such research should be (1) who is labeling a given act as elder abuse and (2) how does difference in culture and morality influence variation in notions of elder abuse. The exclusion of self-neglect and the focus on conflicts in general are important considerations in how elder abuse is conceived in Norway and, from communication with researchers in Sweden and Finland, also in the other Nordic countries (Tornstam, 1989; Saveman et al., 1992, 1993; Virjo, 1992; Kivelä 1993).

Key Problem Number 2: Barriers of Privacy

As noted above, the definitional problems related to family have not received much attention. Why single out the family when so many elderly live in permanent anguish of attack and robbery from strangers in the home and/or on the streets? The obvious reasons are related to the lasting quality of family abuse, the intimate relation between victim and perpetrator, and the secluded nature of privacy. Even though these reasons may seem self-evident, the implications need to be scrutinized.

Through research, the authors have become acutely aware of the complications resulting from the division between the private and public sectors in Norwegian society. This division creates barriers obstructing assistance in several ways. The first barrier is related to the sanctity of privacy. Professionals demonstrate much respect for privacy and are consequently hesitant to interfere. They claim it is hard to find out about conflicts in the family and even harder to intervene in the privacy of people's homes (Hydle & Johns, 1992; Johns et al., 1992; Saveman et al., 1992). The barriers of privacy may take the shape of a closed door, an unanswered telephone call, the practitioner's ignorance of how injuries really have been caused, or a family member refusing admission. Practitioners (particularly social workers) write about how to overcome this problem, but there seems to be a gap between practice and research. Researchers should try to understand such problems to assist in improving measures and methods of intervention. Whether professionals should be given wider legal rights to infringe on privacy is one topic for research and discussion.

Key Problem Number 3: Barriers of Bureaucracy

The division between the private and public sectors creates a barrier in another way. The bureaucratic organization and the professional nature of health and social services inhibit persons from seeking help. With the establishment of specialized services and reporting systems, obtaining assistance has been facilitated in the U.S. Surprisingly to some, seeking help seems to be more complicated in the welfare state. In Norway, there are numerous well-developed institutions that specialize in services for the elderly, all of which are able to help victims of elder abuse. However, elder abuse is not entitled to any special priority or attention. Everybody at the outset is equally entitled to help; *priority* is a problem at all levels of the welfare bureaucracy. The suffering person has to convince the doctor, nurse, or social worker that he or she is sufficiently in need of their help. For most people, this action is not a serious problem. But elderly victims of family abuse are generally very weak clients, their problems are often elusive or concealed, and their symptoms may be vague and ambiguous. Simultaneously, they need help from several different agencies and do not know how to define and prove their needs in a convincing manner. Some of them are too ashamed to even try (Johns et al., 1992.) The organizational barriers they meet may take the shape of counters and bars in the offices, limited opening hours, a long wait/delay (days and weeks) for an appointment, and the lack of knowledge among professionals. Because elder abuse is a complex problem, consultations repeatedly end with a referral to another service. Victims interpret this as a rejection and give up. Several used the expression, "I met the wall" (Hydle & Johns 1992).

Within the bureaucracy of care is a third set of barriers that hinder cooperation, coordination, and exchange of information. The barriers partly arise out of division between professional groups. Nurses and social workers, for example, may have a different understanding of problems and different attitudes towards intervention. They also work with different, and sometimes conflicting, clients. The social worker might try to help an alcoholic, while his old mother is a patient for the home nurses. The police may serve as an example of a third profession that does not cooperate easily with either nurse or social worker. This difference between professional groups is increased by their location in different, rather self-contained, institutions (Johns et al., 1992). The lack of flexible, client-oriented and interdisciplinary action does not imply a lack of resources, but the lack of systematic knowledge about (and specialization of) the problem of elder abuse. Consequently, in spite of a welfare society, victims do not always receive the necessary help.

The Measures: Exploiting Current
Resources Through Mediation

There are no specialized Protective Acts or Mandatory Reporting Acts for adults in Norway. The creation of such acts are unlikely, even though elder abuse is now recognized as a problem. Thus, some kind of specialized education and specific measures are needed, especially considering the complexity of the problem, its inherent dilemmas, and the need to mobilize existing resources. The problem amounts to connecting client and helpers in an effective coalition. There is a need to build bridges over the administrative gaps and "unlock doors" to professional barriers. The answer can be found in the central task of the (U.S.) Adult Protective Service worker as a *mediator*. Such an individual is a social worker who skillfully relates to the needs of the victim and negotiates coordinated service plans (Dolon & Blakely, 1989; Hwalek et al., 1991; Johns et al., 1992).

The authors are assessing a model project called "Protection for the Elderly," located at a Senior Citizen Center in Manglerud, a community within Oslo, the capital and largest city of Norway. Of Oslo's 450,000 inhabitants, approximately 12,000 live in Manglerud (2,500 are age 67 years and older). The population is dense and mostly suburban in character. Generally, Manglerud can be described as a well-integrated, well-administered, and well-equipped community. Most offices and institutions are within walking distance of each other. Local resources available to the elderly comprise a health and social office, several general practitioners, sheltered housing, a day care center, a long-term geriatric ward, a senior citizen center, home nurses and home help office, and police. Other important institutions are located on the secondary level outside the community, such as the hospital, family counselling service, outpatient psychiatric clinic, clinic for alcoholics, women's shelter, and an acute care unit (medical and social).

Considering the number and kinds of institutions, resources for intervention in cases of elder abuse should be there already. The problem is how to engage them. The task of the elder protective social worker is not to work as a specialist taking over cases but in her position at the senior center to function freely as a key-person, reaching out to victims and collaborating with the health and social service professionals. The social worker has a wide-ranging mandate to contact, motivate, and coordinate all relevant resources and services that could contribute to solutions. That person must work towards mobilization, coordination, and adaption of measures to the individual victim. By focusing on victim-support, mediation, and coordination, the project is designed specifically to deal with abuse and neglect.

The project is directed towards developing methods for future work on an extended scale. Based on the various methods of social work, the project aims at developing community-work, family therapy, and advocacy for more systematic mediation between client and professional helpers (Johns et al., 1992). In evaluating the development of elder protective services in Norway, a holistic but localized point of departure is taken. All cases are recorded (not initially excluding non-abuse cases) and the practical consequences of methods for intervention tested. The cause(s) of each case is analyzed while taking care of the victim and offering the best possible help and assistance. Some of the (former) victims will become valuable advisors and assistants in education, research, and policy-making for the project.

THE FUTURE OF THE AGED IN NORWAY AND 'ELDER PROTECTIVE SERVICES'

The general level of violence and conflict seems to be rising with the increasing modernization in Norway. Combined with the increase in the elderly population and the heightened awareness about elder abuse, an increase in the (known) extent and importance of elder abuse may be anticipated. When considering future trends, the first scenario pictures a general increase in abuse. On the other hand, many conflicts are taken care of before family members grow old. Women's liberation and the increase in divorces especially make a difference. Currently, at least one-third of elder abuse cases in Norway seem to be spousal abuse. Advances in child protection and the general development of family therapy might relieve tension in aging families. Thus a second scenario might be a decrease in the family conflict which leads to abuse. However, considering the increase in frail, single, and vulnerable elderly abandoned by family and turned down by hard pressed public services, this scenario may turn out as a change more in the pattern than the extent of elder abuse. An added factor in each scenario might be an increase in crime and abuse from criminals (strangers) in the home. As elder abuse is currently defined, such crime more or less falls outside the topic.

The direction of future changes in the problem of elder abuse will, of course, depend upon much more basic changes in society. In the Scandinavian countries, there is currently a decline in the welfare system, caused by economic depression, with general cuts in all public spending (including health and social care for the elderly). At the same time, the rise of unemployment and (relative) poverty in the population seems to cause greater stress in families. It seems rather obvious that these general trends will affect the situation of the elderly in a negative way. Still, in spite of this rather pessimistic outlook, there is at least one positive trend. The development and spread of knowledge, awareness, and intervention programs for elderly victims of abuse are receiving firm support. There is a general positive attitude in the population, within health and social services, and proper funding from the Ministry of Social Affairs. A national center of violence in now being planned, concentrating on the victimization of larger groups in society.

The future may seem insecure, but Norwegians are, at least, able to work towards increasing the ability to deal with the problems of elder abuse and related aspects of family violence.

REFERENCES

Bennett, G. (1990). Action on elder abuse in the 90's: New definition will help. *Geriatric Medicine, 20* (4), 53-54.

Council of Europe. (1992). *Violence against elderly people.* Strasbourg: Council of Europe Press.

Eastman, M. (1984). *Old age abuse.* London: Age Concern.

Decalmer, P. & Glendenning, F. (eds.) (1993). *The mistreatment of elderly people.* London: SAGE Publications.

Dolon R. & Blakely B.E. (1989). Elder abuse and neglect: A study of adult protective service workers in the United States. *J. Elder Abuse & Neglect, 1*(3), 31-51.

Fulmer, T.T. & O'Malley T.A. (1987). *Inadequate care of the elderly.* New York: Springer.

Gullestad, M. (1991). Doing interpretive analysis in a modern large scale society: The meaning of peace and quiet in Norway. *Social Analysis,* 38-61.

Helset, A. (ed.) (1991). *Elderly women in the Nordic countries* (English summary), Norwegian Institute of Gerontology 6/91, Oslo.

Hugonot, R. (1990). *Violences contre les vieux.* Toulouse: Editions érès.

Hudson M. (1991). Elder mistreatment: A taxonomy of definitions by Delphi. *Journal of Elder Abuse & Neglect, 3*(2), 1-21.

Hwalek M., Williamson D., & Stahl C. (1991). Community-based M-team roles: a job analysis. *Journal of Elder Abuse & Neglect, 3,* 45-73.

Hydle, I. (1989). Violence against the elderly in Western Europe–Treatment and preventive measures in the health and social fields. *Journal of Elder Abuse & Neglect, 1*(3), 75-87.

Hydle, I. & Johns, S. (1992). *Closed doors and clenched fists: When elderly people are abused in their homes* (Norwegian: stengte dører og knyttede never: Når eldre blir utsatt for overgrep i hjemmet) Kommuneforlaget, Oslo.

Johns, S. Hydle I. & Aschjem, Ø. (1991). The act of abuse: A two-headed monster of injury and offense. *Journal of Elder Abuse & Neglect, 3*(1), 53-64.

Johns, S, Juklestad, O., Hydle, I. (1992). Developing elder protective services in Norway. Paper presented at *The Ninth Annual Adult Protective Services Conference,* San Antonio, Texas.

Johnson, T. (1986). Critical issues in the definition of elder abuse, in Pillemer & Wolf (eds.) *Elder Abuse: Conflict in the Family.* Dover, MA: Auburn House.

Kivelä, S.L. (1992). Abuse in old age: Epidemiological data from Finland. *Journal of Elder Abuse & Neglect, 4*(2), 1-18.

Kosberg, J. & Cairl, R. (1986). The cost of care index: A case management tool for screening informal care providers. *The Gerontologist, 26,* 273-278.

NOU (Norwegian Government Report) 1992/1 *Safety-Dignity-Care* (Norwegian: Trygghet-Verdighet-Omsorg), The Ministry of Social Affairs, Oslo.

Pillemer, K.A. & Wolf, R.S. (1986). *Elder abuse: Conflict in the family.* Dover, MA: Auburn House Publishing Company.

Pritchard, J. (1992). *The Abuse of Elderly People: A Handbook for Professionals.* London: Jessica Kingsley Publishers.

Riches, D. (1986) The phenomenon of violence in D. Riches (ed.) *The Anthropology of Violence.* Oxford: Basil Blackwell.

Saveman, B.I. Hallberg, I.R. & Norberg, A. (1993). Identifying/Defining elder abuse, as seen by witnesses. *Journal of Advanced Nursing* (accepted for publication).

Saveman, B.I. Hallberg, I.R. Norberg, A. & Eriksson S. (1993). Patterns of abuse of the elderly in their own homes as reported by district nurses. *Scand J Primary Health Care* (in press).

Saveman, B.I. Norberg, A. & Hallberg I.R. (1992). The problems of dealing with abuse and neglect of the elderly: Interviews with district nurses. *Qual. Health Research, 2*(3), 302-17.

Stang, G. & Evensen Å.R. (1985). Focus on elder abuse (Norwegian: Eldrdemi-shandling frem i lyset) *J. Norwegian Medical Society, 105,* 2475-8.

Stang, G. & Hydle, I. (1986). Elder abuse and neglect–public responsibility (Norw: Mishandling og vanskøtsel av eldre–et offentlig problem) *Ministry of Social Affairs,* 9/86.

Tornstam, L.(1989). Abuse of elderly in Denmark and Sweden. Results from a population study. *Journal of Elder Abuse & Neglect, 1*(1), 35-44.

Tornstam, L. (1992). The quo vadis of gerontology: On the gerontological research paradigm. *The Gerontologist, 32*(3) 318-326.

Virjo, I. (1992). Abuse of the elderly in two rural communes in Southern Finland. Paper to WONCA (The World Organization of Family Doctors), Vancouver 1992.

Chapter 10

Elder Abuse and Neglect in Poland

Małgorzata Halicka, PhD

BACKGROUND

Poland is a country with a rate of demographic aging similar to other developed nations. In 1991, the percentage of persons 60 years and older constituted 15.2 percent of the total population. From year to year the proportion of retired people increases (retirement is age 60 for women and 65 for men). Demographic predictions show further growth in the percentage of people 60 years and older, reaching 18 percent in the year 2000 (Rosset, 1974). At the same time, the proportion of people in the early old age group (below 75 years of age) to the late old age group (above 75 years of age) is changing. Similar to other countries, this is due mostly to the increase of people in late old age, a consequence of prolonging the lifespan and shifting the process of dying to later years.

The aging of the Polish population is specific both in its social and individual dimensions. The typical phenomenon of demographic changes in Poland is the increased rate of aging of the rural society (16.5%) compared to the urban society (12.8%), a result of intensive migration processes of young people moving from the

Małgorzata Halicka is affiliated with the Department of Gerontology, University School of Medicine, 1, Kilinski str. 15-230 Bialystok, Poland.

[Haworth co-indexing entry note]: "Elder Abuse and Neglect in Poland." Halicka, Małgorzata. Co-published simultaneously in the *Journal of Elder Abuse & Neglect* (The Haworth Press, Inc.) Vol. 6, No. 3/4, 1995, pp. 157-169; and: *Elder Abuse: International and Cross-Cultural Perspectives* (ed: Jordan I. Kosberg, and Juanita L. Garcia) The Haworth Press, Inc., 1995, pp. 157-169. Multiple copies of this article/chapter may be purchased from The Haworth Document Delivery Center [1-800-3-HA-WORTH; 9:00 a.m. - 5:00 p.m. (EST)].

country to the city. Polish agriculture is mainly based on small farms ranging from a few to a few dozen hectares. The process of aging is most advanced in this group. Among the old people making their living in farming, one can observe a high percentage of actively working persons. In 1988, among the people over 60 years old, a mere 12 percent in cities were working actively in comparison with 43.5 percent in the country (Rocznik Statystyczny, 1991).

Another feature of demographic changes in Poland is the longer lifespan of women (eight years on the average) in comparison with men that has resulted in a growing majority of women; hence, the problem of widowhood and loneliness. Data analyses also point to that phenomenon. Among men in their sixties or older, the widowers constitute 13.7 percent while widows exceed 50 percent (Rocznik, 1991). The majority of single people are also women: 25 percent single retired women as compared to only 5.9 percent single retired men in the same age group (Synak, 1989).

As far as the structure of education is concerned, the majority of elderly Poles have an elementary education (53.5%). One out of five has not completed elementary level education (20.6%) but one out of five has completed secondary education (15.3%). Those with university education constitute 3.3 percent of the older population (Synak, 1989). Regarding health, a study carried out by the Central Statistical Office revealed that the state of health of old people in Poland is rated as ordinary (51.0 percent) or bad (29.4 percent). Regular or frequent ailments are reported by 60.3 percent of women and 47.6 percent of men.

In analyzing the situation of old people in Poland, it is necessary to consider flat-sharing by young and old people, a characteristic of the Polish family model. The tradition of generations living under one roof is strongly rooted in the mentality of the Polish society and occurs more frequently than in highly industrialized countries. Among the 65 year olds, 67 percent live together with children and grandchildren (Piotrowski, 1973). The percentage of multi-generation families living under one roof in Polish cities and villages is different. It depends, partly, on the level of industrialization of a given region, financial state of particular families, and cultural background. It is difficult to know what influences this particular characteristic of a Polish family, whether it is objective conditioning or personal factors (like the sense of strong ties between generations). Most certainly, housing problems are one cause of that state of affairs.

In Poland, hardly any newly-wedded couple has its own flat and most often they live with the parents of the husband or wife for the first few years. It often happens that aging parents live together with their children in order to help run the house and look after the grandchildren (whose parents are working). The multi-generation structure of most Polish families results from necessity rather than from a conscious choice. It should be emphasized that the economic situation for retired people is difficult in Poland and is due to both the policy of a socialist country (carried out for the last 40 years) and difficult economic situations. Low pensions are the sole source of maintenance, making it difficult for an aged person to meet the basic needs. This factor favors the maintenance of multi-generation families.

The complexity of the elderly's life situations in Poland increases the probability that they will be subject to neglect and abuse. However, the problem of neglect and abuse of the elderly has not yet been identified. Individual studies (Tryfam, 1968; Synak, 1982, 1990) only marginally suggest the existence of the phenomenon. Thus, it is difficult to estimate the extent of the problem in Poland. The lack of information in Polish gerontology must be kept in mind. This chapter presents basic material from an environmental research study carried out by the Gerontology Department of the Medical University School in Bialystok within the past few years. The research concerned the problem of neglect and abuse of the elderly people (Halicka, 1992) among the citizens of a big city, and so it cannot be generalized to rural areas.

Polish gerontological literature has not defined abuse and neglect with regard to the elderly people. The definition given by Harris (1988), "Misuse of power resulting in a reduction of the quality of an elderly person's life," is considered to be too general. Thus, the following interpretation of "neglect" and "abuse" is presented:

Neglect is a more or less conscious activity aimed at harmful treatment of the elderly person manifested by the refusal to provide the necessary help. Neglect may occur in the psychological sphere (e.g., insufficient attention, care, isolation), in the material sphere (e.g., lack of basic maintenance) and in the health sphere (e.g., lack of health care, nursing during illness).

Abuse has a double meaning: in the material sphere, it consists of taking advantage of the elderly person (e.g., stealing money, inappropriately using funds, and uncontrolled profiting from properties) and in the physical sphere by acts of aggression or violence in terms of mistreatment (physical and/or psychological).

STUDY PRESENTATION

The study presented in this chapter was carried out in the city of Bialystok in 1989. A cohort method was used, comparing six groups from the cohorts of 60, 70, and 80-year old men and women. Altogether 600 inhabitants of Bialystok have been included in the study questionnaire.

Bialystok is a city in northeastern Poland presently inhabited by over 270,000 people of very heterogeneous backgrounds in terms of customs and traditions. The elderly citizens of Bialystok mostly came to the city seeking employment, but there is also a group who moved when they retired to join their children and grandchildren. Hence, the elderly population of Bialystok consists of three sub-groups: (a) those born in Bialystok; (b) those born and raised in villages, who moved to Bialystok in their youth and worked in the city (early employment migration); and (c) those who came to the city in their old age to live with their children (late post-employment migration). The traditions brought over from the rural world influence the lifestyle within the city. One such tradition is a strong sense of union within the family and between generations.

Social Reality as a Source of Neglect and Abuse

This study presents the opinions of elderly people about contemporary customs. More than 80 percent of those questioned, both women and men, claim that manners are worse than they used to be.

Among those people who negatively rated present day manners is a group who personally were harmed by other people (Figure 1), most often men and women in their 80s. Undoubtedly, their own negative life experiences have a direct influence on shaping their opinions. However, the majority of people negatively evaluating contemporary manners did not experience personal harm and, yet, tend to have a critical attitude towards the present age. This reflects a conservative attitude toward contemporary manners which is typical for many elderly people. Keep in mind the fact that in the past the influence of elderly people on shaping attitudes used to be quite positive. Now, it has been reduced as a result of the reshaping of the Polish model of the family and the rapid change of customs. All those changes can justify the feeling of imminent danger and threats, even if they are symbolic or irrational. The reality, alien and remote, becomes still less understood and more dangerous.

The analysis of data confirms the feeling that exists among the

FIGURE 1. Evaluation of Contemporary Manners and the Experience of Personal Harm.

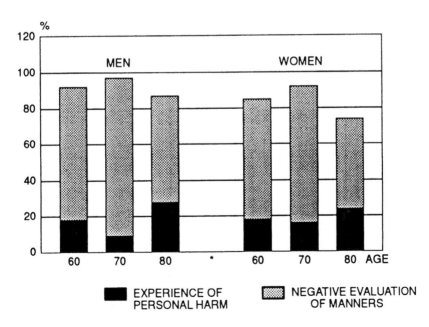

retired people of real or perceived danger connected with the outside world. Those interviewed were asked if they felt anxious or threatened when staying alone at home or when leaving the house at different times of the day and night. As can be noted on Fig. 2, 7 to 28 percent of those questioned were afraid to leave their flats during the day and about 20 to 70 percent feared leaving in the evening or at night. The percentage of those who are fearful about going out at night increased with age and is greater among women. In the younger age groups, the apprehension of leaving home resulted most often from the fears of being assaulted (51 percent of 60-year old women). In the older age groups, the fears were mostly connected with anxieties about the negative impact on their health (about 20 percent).

Growing older increases the percentage of people who are afraid to stay at home alone (7 to 17 percent among men, depending on the age group, and from 15 in the youngest to 32 in the oldest group of

FIGURE 2. The Sense of Insecurity in Elderly People About Leaving Their Homes.

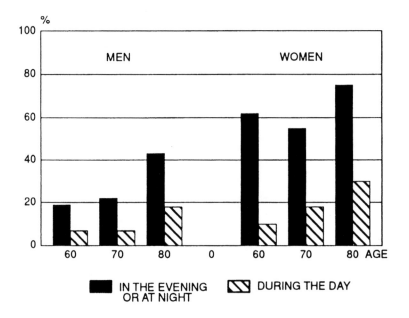

women). The causes of fear among the people staying alone at home relate mainly to fears of being assaulted or beaten, declining health, and concern about their property.

The frequent sense of impending danger is, as indicated earlier, the consequence of harm experienced in younger years. About 20 percent of the respondents, depending on sex and age group, experienced various kinds of victimization from other people. The following are some utterances of those questioned: "I was assaulted, beaten, and robbed" (60-year old man), "While drinking alcohol in a company of others, I was beaten many times by my companions" (70-year old man), "At dark, when I was on the street, some hooligans hit me on the head and took my watch" (80-year old man), "In my own flat, I was assaulted and stabbed three times" (80-year old man), "Insults, helplessness, mocking the elderly people who are less efficient" (60-year old woman), "Frequent rows with drunkards renting flats" (70-year old woman), "The customers do not always pay for sewing a dress" (80-year old woman).

The research findings point to the fact that strangers were the source of threat and abuse for only a small percentage of the questioned elderly people. Most often abuse was physical aggression (7 percent of men and from 4 percent among the youngest to 60 percent among the oldest women). Only 4 percent of women encountered emotional aggression. One can assume that the acts of aggression concerned mainly marginal groups of society or people indulging too freely in alcohol. Since one of the situations associated with the release of aggression is alcohol drinking, a special research study was conducted aimed at examining alcohol consumption and alcoholism among the elderly.

Drinking small amounts of alcohol is common and is more likely to involve men than women. Drinking high-grade alcohol (e.g., vodka with 40 percent alcohol) is typical in this geographical area. Imbibing more than 250 g on single occasions was common for 34 percent of 60 year-olds and 15 percent of older men. This form of alcohol drinking, not found among women, does not differ from the practice of the younger age groups. Alcohol addiction was noted among 3.3 percent of the people questioned; mostly those in the 60 year-old cohort. It should be noted here that excessive alcohol consumption was encountered in the group that was interviewed and those closest to them (family, neighbors). In their families, there were cases of alcohol addiction ranging from 5 to 14 percent, depending on the age group. In single cases, the stealing of money (most often by a son) for alcohol was found. Thus, it seems, that excessive alcohol consumption, in the environment of the elderly, constitutes one of the important risk factors in their abuse.

Family as a Source of Neglect and Abuse

It is not only the social environment, but also home and family, that could be a source of fear and violence for the elderly person. As mentioned, the elderly people in Poland often live with their families which can create conflicts. Although the family atmosphere was proper in a majority of the cases, there were various occasions of neglect associated with conflict. When questioned about neglect in the psychological, material, and care spheres, 50 to 90 percent of the elderly persons did not report any neglect by the younger family members. The lack of psychological support was reported by less than 10 percent. Only in the cohort of 90 year-old women did it reach 14 percent. The lack of material support did not exceed 7 percent. Frequent or sporadic lack of care was reported by 5 percent of 60 year-old to 21 percent of 70 year-old men and about 12 percent of women in different age cohorts; 5 to 13 percent reported being isolated from family affairs (Figure 3). All forms of neglect appeared to be more frequent in the late age cohort. It should be noted that about 15 percent claimed that they did not need any family support.

Conflicts among the family members were more frequent (16 to 36 percent) but were mostly sporadic. The party who was striving to dominate and impose the attitudes (or patterns of behavior) was most frequently a spouse, rarely children or other family members. The son-in-law or daughter-in-law as the cause of conflict was seldom reported, except for the cohort of 70 year-old women (who in 11 out of 100 cases claimed that their son-in-law or daughter-in-law caused the conflict). The forms of the family conflicts varied. There were most often a few days of mutual silence between the parties (4-15 percent); shouting and other verbal offenses were rarer, less than 10 percent.

In quarreling families, acts of aggression were directed against

FIGURE 3. Neglect by the Family.

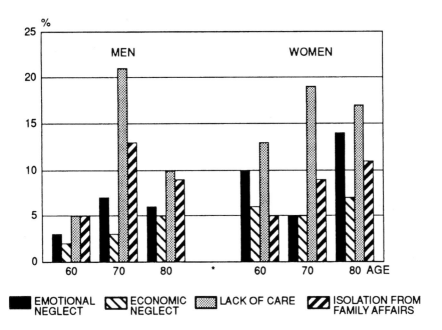

EMOTIONAL NEGLECT   ECONOMIC NEGLECT   LACK OF CARE   ISOLATION FROM FAMILY AFFAIRS

older men. The cases of open aggression, both physical and psychological, were observed in a few percent in each age group. At the same time, the psychological abuse (e.g., shouts, other offenses) were more frequent than physical violence.

Elderly people living with their families were sometimes subject to material abuse. Examples included the free use of their property, inappropriate use of their money, and robbery. The frequency of these abuses was not high, and together did not exceed 12 percent (except the cohort of 80 year-old women of whom 19 percent were the victims of material abuse) (Figure 4). These abuses were often directed towards people who were physically or materially dependent on younger family members.

Various conflicts, threats, and fears could be the cause of suicidal ideation; yet, such thoughts appeared rarely among the respondents, in less than 7 percent for each age cohort. The men in the 60 year-old cohort were twice as likely to report suicidal thoughts

FIGURE 4. Elderly as Victims of Abuse.

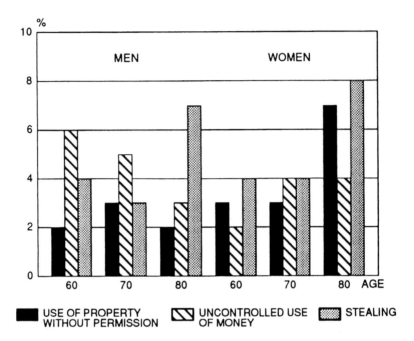

which could be explained by the active work life of this group. Considering the frequency of depressive states caused by arteriosclerotic dementia, suicidal thoughts cannot all be attributed to family conflicts (Rembowski, 1984).

Old people with chronic diseases, especially in later stages, are dependent on other people for care; in Poland most often from a spouse or other family members. Neglecting the care of older people could worsen the quality of life. The subjects were asked the question: "Whose help can you count on in the case of sudden illness?" The majority answered that they relied on a spouse or on children. These answers are a positive indication of the emotional bonds in the family. It is worth mentioning that 20 to 50 percent of those questioned also counted on the help of their neighbors or friends; only a few percent relied on nurses or other professional carers.

DISCUSSION

In recapitulating the research findings, it can be stated that the frequency of conflicts, especially direct physical aggression, was not high. The threat of physical aggression was greater outside the family while psychological aggression occurred more often within the family. Family conflicts were mostly sporadic which points to the durability of family ties. No clear correlation between the occurrence of conflicts and social class and education was found. The existence of family and intergenerational conflicts, on a scale, as a widespread social pathology, was not confirmed.

Similar observations were made by others (Piotrowski, 1973; Dyczewski, 1976, 1981; Suslowska 1989). It is important to note the influence of the residence on the creation, course, and results of family conflicts. In cities, neglect and abuse of the elderly are more frequently the result of a shortage of flats, lack of specified social roles for old people, their dependency in terms of care and help, and alcohol abuse. Conflict between parents and children in the rural societies is a result of life in those societies where housekeeping is inseparably connected with farming which means common work (Synak, 1983; Tryfan, 1992). It does not, however, mean that the generational ties in a Polish family either in the city or the country have deteriorated. The fundamental elements of reshaping the Polish model of the family are changes in the cohesion within the families. The personal ties dominate over the structural and objective bonds.

The years of economic crisis in Poland and radical contemporary political and economic changes affect many social groups, creating a threat especially for elderly people. It is worth mentioning the growth of delinquency during the economic crisis (seen in the statistics). Moreover, the elderly and lonely people very often become the victims of the delinquents. On the other hand, the circumstances favoring the conflicts and tension, neglect, and abuses within the generational community result from the shortage of flats, excessive duties (also in the case of the oldest generation), and lengthening the time necessary for the young people to become independent and self-sufficient.

It is not only the social environment and family, but also the loneliness, that can constitute a threat for an elderly person. A lonely life can lead to depression, hostile self-attitudes, alcoholism, or addiction to medication. These social, domestic, and personal situations can be the source of threats, neglect, and abuse. The factors creating this state can be different: the impairment of an individual that results in limitations in self-defense and mobility, a worsening state of health, loneliness, property, and in living in the old districts of the city (where the old housing structures help to create social pathology) (Ciesla, 1983; Teorie socjologii miasta . . ., 1983).

There are various circumstances leading to tensions, conflicts, neglect, abuse, physical violence and psychological ill-treatment of the old people. The neglect of elderly people by the younger family members can result from too many duties, both at home and work. The problem of care is not only a matter of family obligations, but it should also be the activity of social care services which were created for that purpose.

The (malfunctioning) social services in Poland do not solve the problems of the elderly people. The transition from the centrally-managed economy to the market economy means that there is a necessity of forming a new model of social services which will account for the changes in the functioning of the economic system, the ways of governing the country, patronage system, and solving conflicting situations. The following are potential activities for policies and programs aimed at preventing and solving the problems of neglect:

- Development of more varied and effective systems of social help enabling full housing and material self-sufficiency in conflicting families;
- Improvement of the retired people's economic situation in order to limit their financial dependency on the family;
- More efficient implementation of activities to fight alcoholism;
- Provision of life-long education that will prepare old people for retirement and acceptance of the progression of age;
- Introduction of self-help organizations;
- Creation of an attitude of solidarity between society and elderly people in opposition to violence; and
- Cooperation with the church in shaping attitudes toward old people, improvement in manners, and prevention of neglect and abuse.

REFERENCES

Bień, B. Halicka M.: "Konsumpcja alkoholu i alkoholizm ludzi starych" in "Progranicze"–Studia Społeczne 1992 vol. I, pp. 105-109.

Cieśla, S.: "Stare dzielnice mieszkaniowe: środowisko mieszkalne i społeczne" in "Roczniki Nauk Społecznych" 1983 vol. II pp. 185-198.

Dyczewski, L.: "Więz pokoleń w rodzinie"–Warszawa: ODiSS, 1976.

Dyczewski, L.: "Rodzine polska i kierunki jej przemian"–Warszawa: ODiSS, 1981.

Halicka, M.: "Ludzie starzy jako podmiot i przedmiot patologii społecznej" ("Old people As A Subject And Object of Social Pathology")–Lublin (Katolicki Uniwersytet Lubelski) 1992.–The doctorate thesis in the archives of The Gerontology Department of the Medical University in Białystok.

Harris, C.: "Abuse Of The Elderly." "Brit. Med. J." 1988, pp. 293, 813.

Piotrowski, J.: "Miejsce człowieka starego w rodzinie i społeczeństwie"–Warszawa: PWN, 1973.

Rembowski, J.: "Psychologiczne problemy starzenia sięczlowieka"–Warszawa-Poznań: PWN, 1984.

Rocznik Statystyczny–Warszawa: GUS, 1991.

Rosset, E.: "Starzenie się społeczeństw–problem demograficzny XX wieku" in "Problemy ludzi starych w Polsce"–Warszawa: PWE, 1974 pp. 9-50.

Synak, B.: "Sytuacja starych rodziców mieszkających u dzieci w miescie" in "Problemy rodziny" 1985, number 4.

Synak, B.: "Człowiek stary w zmienionym kontekście rodzinnym" in "Gdańskie Zeszyty Humanistyczne" 1985, number 29.

Synak, B.: "The Polish family: Stability, change and conflicts" in "Journal of Aging Studies" 1990 vol. 3, number 4, pp. 333-344.

Synak, B.: Sytuacja bytowa ludzi starych w 1989 r. "Warszawa: GUS, 1990.

Susłowska, M.: "Psychologia starzenia się i starości" Warszawa: PWN, 1989.

"Teorie socjologii miasta a problemy społeczne miast polskich"–ed. E. Kaltenberg-Kwiatkowska (and others) Wrocław: Ossolineum, 1983.

Tryfan, B.: "Niektóre aspekty konfliktów o ziemię" in "Wieśwspółczesna" 1968, number 12.

Tryfan, B.: "Rola rodziny w życiu człowieka starego na wsi" in "Refleksje nad starością–aspekty społeczne, edukacyjne i etyczne. Pamiętnik sympozjum PTG" Lóz 1992 pp. 59-66.

Chapter 11

Elder Abuse in South Africa

S. C. A. Eckley, MSocSc
P. A. C. Vilakazi, BA (SW)

INTRODUCTION

Abuse, ill-treatment, and victimization of older persons are growing phenomena in South Africa, demanding greater public attention and response in recent years. It is still not known whether the interest is evoked by an actual increase of abuse incidents, larger numbers of older citizens, changing family and community values, or sensational reports in the media. In this chapter, the problem of elder abuse within the South African context will be examined.

It is important to understand at the outset that the abuse within families or institutions in South Africa is not much different from most other countries as seen in research reports or books. However, from a sociopolitical perspective, elder abuse in South Africa takes on unique and extraordinary characteristics. Basically, this characterization refers to institutionalized and even legalized racial discrimination called Apartheid. As a direct result of Apartheid (meaning separateness), family and community life disintegrated when

S. C. A. Eckley is Executive Director and P. A. C. Vilakazi is Director of Information and Education of the South African Council for the Aged, 45 on Castle, Cape Town, 8001.

[Haworth co-indexing entry note]: "Elder Abuse in South Africa." Eckley, S. C. A., and P. A. C. Vilakazi. Co-published simultaneously in the *Journal of Elder Abuse & Neglect* (The Haworth Press, Inc.) Vol. 6, No. 3/4, 1995, pp. 171-182; and: *Elder Abuse: International and Cross-Cultural Perspectives* (ed: Jordan I. Kosberg, and Juanita L. Garcia) The Haworth Press, Inc., 1995, pp. 171-182. Multiple copies of this article/chapter may be purchased from The Haworth Document Delivery Center [1-800-3-HAWORTH; 9:00 a.m. - 5:00 p.m. (EST)].

171

black workers, who flocked to cities to find work, were not allowed to bring their families with them. This practice destroyed the social fabric and values that give meaning to caring about others, especially the elderly. It is, therefore, understandable that the disenfranchised people started to fight for human freedoms and their rights, while the privileged ones fought back to retain their supremacy. The tragic result is that South Africa has been regarded as possibly one of the most violent countries in the world. Violence has become a way of life.

In 1981, the South African Council for the Aged was the first body to speak out against abuse of older persons and sought action by the authorities and public. Seminars were held throughout the country (Droskie, 1981). However, little public interest was generated, and limited research undertaken. In 1992, a seminar on abuse in old age homes, organized by the Centre of Gerontology in Cape Town, stirred much interest which resulted in a public debate on the subject (Conradie & Charlton, 1992). Abuse of residents in homes for the aged has became a focal point of interest. Although attempts to force the Government to institute a full-scale inquiry have not yet been successful, the level of awareness has been raised. An organization, called The Friends of Abused Frail Elderly in Homes, was formed in 1992.

The extent of the problem of elder abuse in South Africa has not yet been scientifically established. The fact that there is no central register for elder abuse or an elder help line in operation in South Africa also makes it difficult to estimate the extent of the problem. The high level of violence and a general mistrust in the police force compounds the problem. In general, the elderly of South Africa are not sufficiently aware of their rights and how to execute them. The South African Council for the Aged launched the first declaration on the rights of the elderly in October of 1993 and is presently negotiating for the establishment of an ombudsman for seniors with the Government and senior citizen organizations.

The elderly population is expected to increase to 4.3 percent by the year 2010. The most rapid growth increase in numbers will be among black elderly from the present 980,000 to 1.8 million before 2010 (Ferreira, 1992). An important demographic feature is an acceleration of the 80 years and older group. In 1993 there were

150,000 persons at least aged 80, and by 2002 the number will increase to 890,000, almost sixfold. There appears to be a strong correlation between the number of reported incidents of abuse and the advanced age of victims. The more rapid growth rate of the female aged population, compared with the male aged population, is also evident. In 1985, females accounted for 55 to 60 percent of the total elderly population. It is estimated that by 2010, 70 to 75 percent of elderly South Africans will be female.

Present living circumstances of elderly persons require close scrutiny. Diversity is a particular characteristic with white elderly who prefer to live apart from their families, while black elderly choose (or are forced by circumstances) to live with their children. In black townships (ghetto-like environments) elderly normally share two-room houses with between six to ten other persons. In a recent national survey, more than 80 percent of black elderly experienced serious living problems due to lack of basic living conveniences and over-crowding, lack of access to health and other care, and crime and violence (Ferreira et al., 1992). Discrepancies regarding the availability of care facilities for frail and demented elderly between the various racial groups is a unique feature of the South African scene. More than 8 percent of white persons over 65 years live in homes for the aged, while the total number of beds for frail black is 1300, constituting less than 0.5 percent. The implication is clear; frail black elderly are forced to live at home, thus causing tremendous strain on families to provide care. This situation surely breeds elder abuse.

Inequalities and racial discrimination in education and labor opportunities over many years have multiple implications for older South Africans. A national survey found that 50 percent of whites and less than 10 percent of blacks have been employed in the modern economic sector. The vast majority of black elderly have been totally dependent on a social pension provided by the State which, until September 1993, was approximately 40 percent less than received by whites. In communities with high levels of unemployment (and consequent poverty), heavy demands and pressure are placed on elderly who receive social pensions. Despite the stressful circumstances under which the majority of the elderly in South Africa live, younger and older generations continue to support one another. Evidence is clearly on the side of the multigenerational vigor and positive quality of family in South Africa.

ETIOLOGY AND NATURE OF ELDER ABUSE IN SOUTH AFRICA

A clear conceptualization of elder abuse, neglect, or victimization enhances the development of theory, diagnostic instruments, preventative and treatment policies and strategies. Existing definitions of elder abuse seem to highlight the taboo nature of the subject. Professionals and the general public alike either do not believe it exists or refuse to accept that it is a reality. The South African Council for the Aged defines elder abuse as both deliberate and unintentional maltreatment (physical, emotional, social or financial), of any elderly person (Eckley, 1983). It is destructive behavior that causes suffering to the elderly person.

The reviews of research and other literature indicate no single explanation for mistreatment of elderly persons. Until now, no comprehensive study has been undertaken to determine causes for elder abuse in South Africa. In the evaluation of case experiences and incidents, it was found that the problems of elder abuse could be attributed to multiple causes, ranging from personal, environmental, economical, to traditional reasons. The following are basic explanations for elder abuse in South Africa.

Etiology of Elder Abuse

Pathological Behavior. A pathological framework explains mistreatment of the elderly in terms of personal problems inherent in the abuser. Elderly persons become vulnerable to abuse because of their proximity and visibility to and their dependency on, people with pathological behavior problems (Eckley, 1991). The situation is aggravated by excessive demands on carers who cannot cope, resulting in negative behavior patterns. For example, a 13 year-old boy was forced to stay at home caring for a frail elderly family member. His acts of aggression were directly related to his inability to deal with the care demands. It has also been found that family members, who are not able to find employment or who have personality problems so that they are unable to hold a job, are frequently assigned the responsibility to care for a frail elder. The authors have found a high percentage of abusers, approximately 25 percent, are alcoholics. In almost 50 percent of cases of abuse at home, the abuser used alcohol before acts of violence. Regarding reported cases of abuse in institutions, a high level of stress and even depression was reported among both victims and abusers.

Interpersonal Relationships. A strong correlation was noted in case studies in South Africa between interpersonal relationships and abuse. It is the experience of the authors that positive, open and mutually-respectful relationships in both institutional and home settings hardly ever lead to abuse. A destructive relationship over many years between parent and child very often results in incidents of abuse in later life.

Developmental Approach. Also referred to as the life-cycle approach, the developmental view regards abusive behavior as a recurring phenomenon within the family. It is suggested that children who have grown up in violent families will more likely develop abusive behavior under stressful circumstances and/or when dependency roles are reversed. A daughter of 45 who frequently "disciplines" her mother of 75 by beating her has failed to accept the fact that it is wrong, although she was brought up this way.

Environmental Approach. Irrational reactions to life crises and unfavorable environmental conditions play an important role in causing elder abuse and neglect. In a South African study on the role of environmental factors, the consistent emerging theme was the perception by both the abuser and the abused that they were victims of situational stresses (Eckley, 1991). The situational factors more frequently identified as causing abuse were sociopolitical, accommodation, financial, public unrest, non-availability of health and social care facilities and services, health status of carers and elderly, and unwanted dependency.

Nature of Elder Abuse

A description of the profiles of the victim, the abuser, and symptoms of mistreatment are important to develop a clear understanding of the problem.

Profile of the Victim. Bristowe and Collins (1989) compared the characteristics of elderly care recipients who were victims of abuse with those who enjoyed abuse-free care. Case studies undertaken by Vilakazi in certain black townships in South Africa correspond well with the Bristowe and Collins findings. The average age of the victims was between 70 and 80 years with a ratio of seven females to one male. They suffered from chronic illnesses, immobility, incontinence, and aphasia. Depression, confusion, dementia, and demanding behavior were present. They had limited financial means, social interactions, living space, care equipment, and community resources. A past history of family violence was also noted. Constant supervision, assistance with daily living requirements, and day and night care were very much needed. It is clear that the potential victim demands a great deal of care and attention from, and is highly dependent on, their caregivers. It must be appreciated that persons in appropriate alternative care may be equally demanding and subject to abuse.

Profile of the Abuser. In the evaluation of case studies in private homes and institutional settings, a number of factors were identified as placing caregivers at-risk of becoming abusers. They were more apt to be between 55 and 60 years old, more often female (55%) than male (45%), and a family member (85%). Feelings of loss of control, depression, confusion, low esteem, resentment, helplessness, and guilt, together with a lack of acknowledgement and support, were present. Other psychological and social factors included constant negative and aggressive communication, accompanied by punishment through hurtful criticism or withdrawal, poor interpersonal relationships, isolation, financial stresses, inadequate housing, lack of appropriate caring skills and supervision, ignorance of needs and resources, and absence of care facilities. Physically, these caregivers show evidence of strain, tiredness, and self-neglect (Eckley, 1991). It is obvious that the care of frail elderly persons places extreme demands and responsibility on a caregiver. In institutional settings, the demands on care staff can also be excessive, especially in the face of inadequate training, supervision, knowledge, and care equipment plus long working hours and staff shortages.

Types of Abuse

The study on forms of abuse by Dolon and Hendricks (1989) correspond well with findings in South Africa. Common forms of abuse are as follows:

- *Physical abuse:* slapping, pushing, hitting, restraining, bruising, burning, cutting, etc.
- *Psychological abuse:* insulting, blaming, ignoring, humiliating, isolating, blackmailing, swearing at, treating as a child or calling names.
- *Material/Financial abuse:* illegal/unethical exploitation of funds, property, assets, pension or other money as well as thefts, fraud and damage.
- *Social/physical isolation:* abandonment, locking away in room.
- *Passive neglect:* Unintentional failure to fulfill care needs e.g. non-provision of food.
- *Active neglect:* Intentional failure to fulfill care needs, e.g., deliberate abandonment and/or denial of food or medicine.
- *Self abuse/neglect:* Abuse of alcohol/drugs, improper diet, failure to care for him/herself.
- *Sexual abuse:* Rape, perversion, molestation.
- *Violation of rights:* Withholding information or dominating to make decisions.
- *Late onset spouse abuse:* Although abuse may have been part of marriage for many years, it can also be triggered late in life because of certain factors, e.g., conflict because of aging, etc.

A 1992 workshop on malpractices and mistreatment of residents of homes for the aged, held in Cape Town, South Africa concluded that a distinction needs to be made between mistreatment and elder abuse. Mistreatment was seen as verbal abuse, passive and active neglect, financial exploitation and over-medication. Abuse was described as physical, psychological, and sexual abuse and theft (Conradie & Charlton, 1992).

Effects of Abuse

The effects of elder abuse are not well researched and documented. Attempts by the South African Council for the Aged to identify critical factors have been unsuccessful, highlighting the fact that the abused are reluctant to share their feelings and experiences with others. The following case studies used by Vilakzai (1993) in her research identify some of the effects of elder abuse.

Sellinah wants to die. Sellinah is 69, immobile, and has lived with her daughter and family since the death of her husband in 1984. She is extremely neglected, dirty and smelly, is chronically ill, receives no medical care and has no contact with outsiders. Investigation by a careworker has also found evidence of financial exploitation. Sellinah refused to talk about the situation, except to say that she wishes to die. She is helpless, lonely, totally neglected, and rejected with no hope for a better life.

Trapped. Susan is 70, lives with a divorced 40-year old daughter who abuses alcohol. Susan is immobile and crawls through the two-room house. The daughter has power of attorney to draw her social pension so she gets "robbed" every month. Susan has not seen a doctor for years; she cannot go outside. There is no electricity and hardly any food, except when provided by strangers. She is locked in the house for as long as five days at a time when the daughter goes to her friends.

Who cares? Mary, 89, lives with two "foster" children, 16 and 19 (whose parents disappeared 15 years ago). She has been caring for them since that time. The house belongs to her and is now totally neglected. About 15 families are squatting in the yard. These lodgers refuse to pay rent. She asked the church minister to help, and he now controls her finances, but never gives her the full amount of her pension. The children are unemployed and have little food to live on. Mary is afraid to ask anybody for help.

PREVENTION AND INTERVENTION

South Africa has been slow in recognizing the extent and significance of elder abuse. The Aged Persons Act of 1967 is outdated and does not even refer to the subject of abuse. In the past year, questions have been raised in Parliament but with little effect. According to Government sources, the Aged Persons Act is to be revised in 1994, following the expected new political dispensation for South Africa ensuring full democratic rights for all.

Barriers to Intervention

In designing a strategy to deal with elder abuse, The South African Council for the Aged identified the following barriers:

* Lack of alternatives to family care and inability to escape.
* Social taboos about invading family privacy.
* Severe emotions involved in reporting an abuser.
* Victims often hiding facts out of fear of further abuse.
* Fear of possible institutionalization.

Further, the fact that the elderly are often house- or bed-bound constrain them from reporting incidents.

Guidelines to Families

Eckley (1983) compiled the following guidelines for families caring for dependent elderly at home:

Decision-making. In view of the wide range of implications for all persons involved, it is necessary that the decision to care for an elder dependent be taken both individually and jointly. The tendency to force the decision on the elderly person, or on other family members, must be avoided at all times.

Contracting. Given the unpredictability of human behavior and changing circumstances and expectations, all parties concerned must negotiate an agreement on matters such as finance, roles and tasks, privacy, and living arrangements. The agreement must be evaluated from time to time and adjusted when necessary. Alternative arrangements need to be identified beforehand.

Independence. It is important to respect and maintain the independence of all persons in the family. This means respect for privacy, relationships, activities and decision-making.

Social interaction. Such interaction, both within the family and outside, should be furthered and maintained. The elder's social contacts with persons outside can provide both personal fulfillment and, at the same time, prevent loneliness and tension within the family. Other family members also need to continue with their normal outside social life. Social interaction within the family must be both informally and formally planned and organized.

Shared tasks. Ordinary tasks in the family need to be shared by all, including the elder. If specific tasks are assigned to the elder, he/she will experience this as meaningful and feel a valued part of the family. The tasks in caring for a frail person need to be shared among family members.

Full day of activities. The daily routine of the elderly person depends on the person's state of health but should provide for maximum and constructive mental, social, and physical involvement and participation. Lack of stimulation and purposeful activities can lead to frustration and isolation.

Relationship-building. As in the case of any family, intrafamily relationships need continuous strengthening. Opportunities should be created for "building bridges" especially between the elderly and younger family members.

Outside support. In caring for a frail elderly person, it is necessary to know where and how outside support can be recruited. The support services normally needed are nursing, day or respite care, consultation, and visiting. Short-term alternative care should also be available when required.

Caregiver Support Programs

The establishment of caregiver support groups and respite care constitute recent developments in South Africa. There are two basic types of caregiver groups: self-help and those that are led by professionals. They are not mutually-exclusive, in that self-help groups often consult professionals and vice versa. Respite care means time off or relief for the regular caregiver or dependent elderly person. In South Africa, respite care is mostly an informal program organized by caregiver groups and churches or amongst relatives and neighbors.

A Preventive Program to Combat Elder Abuse in Institutions

This program, developed by the State and private sector, will be instituted in 1994. The program will make provision for the following:

- Training of staff both professional and non-professional to increase and update levels of knowledge and skill.
- Detection and referral mechanisms to effect methods for the early identification and referral of incidents. Residents and visiting committees, and case conferences are some of the mechanisms to be used.
- A charter of residents' rights is envisaged, backed by an ombudsman who will do the necessary investigations.

Curative Intervention Program

In view of the fact that more than 95 percent of older persons in South Africa live outside institutions, the majority of intervention programs should be community-based. However, community care programs in South Africa are not well-developed, as only 3 percent of elderly in the community receive supportive services (like meals-on-wheels, home-care and transport). Social workers and community nurses play an important role in community care but, due to sociopolitical and financial factors, have not been accessible to the majority of the elderly. Community care programs in South Africa are basically built on so-called Western models.

Since 1981, the South African Council for the Aged initiated an indigenous care model, called the People Empowerment Program. Through the deployment of community workers, local people (especially the elderly), are motivated and equipped to develop service infra-structures in accordance with local needs and resources. Typical service components are luncheon clubs and homecare run by club members and locally trained volunteers. Frail elderly living at home are visited and provided assistance. This informal network has been found to have both preventative and curative qualities.

CLOSING REMARKS

Elder abuse, neglect, and victimization need to be addressed on both the macro and micro levels. On a macro level, attitudes which result in the maltreatment of the elderly can be influenced through increased efforts in community education. Greater awareness and, thus, more accurate identification of the problem of elderly victims can lead to the reshaping of attitudes and the broadening of knowledge about abuse and the required services. Social workers, who of all the helping professions are presently in the widest range of settings serving the elderly, are in a unique position to assume leadership in an effort to further community awareness and action. Finding a working definition for elder abuse appropriate to the South African society is a priority, if the problem is to be successfully addressed. On the micro level, successful preventive and curative intervention require professionals and lay persons to acquire adequate knowledge of this phenomenon. They require knowledge of self, of the dynamics of aging, of abuse within and outside of the family, of cultural and societal influences, of appropriate helping strategies and of the skills to implement such knowledge.

REFERENCES

Bristowe, E. & Collins, J.B. (1989). Family mediated abuse of non-institutionalized frail elderly men and women living in British Columbia. *Journal of Elder Abuse & Neglect, 1*(1), 45-64.

Conradie G. & Charlton, K. (1992). Malpractices and mistreatment of residents of homes for the aged. HSRC/UCT Centre for Gerontology, University of Cape Town.

Dolon, R. & Hendricks, J.E. (1989). An exploratory study comparing attitudes and practices of police officers and social service providers in elder abuse and neglect cases. *Journal of Elder Abuse & Neglect, 1* (1), 75-90.

Droskie, Z.M. (1981). Annual report on the SA National Council for the Aged, SA National Council for the Aged, Cape Town.

Eckley, S.C.A. (1991). Family violence: Abuse of the elderly in B. McKendrick & W. Hoffman (eds.). *People and violence in South Africa*. Cape Town, Oxford University Press.

Eckley, S.C.A. (1983). Die Versorging van die Bejaarde. In benster op die Gesin, J. Krooze (ed.), Potchefstroom: Potchefstrooomse Universiteit vir CHO, 329-33.

Ferreira, M., Moller, V., Prinsloo, F.R., & Gillis, L.S. (1992). Multi-dimensional survey of elderly South Africans, 1990-1991: Key findings. HSRC/UCT Centre for Gerontology, Cape Town.

Vilakazi, P.A. C. (1993). Elder abuse in townships in the Vaal Triangle, Unisa, Pretoria.

Chapter 12

Common and Unique Themes on Elder Abuse from a World-Wide Perspective

Jordan I. Kosberg, PhD
Juanita L. Garcia, EdD

OVERVIEW

Elder abuse is not a phenomenon found only in the U.S., Canada, and Great Britain, nor does it only exist within developed nations in the world. Although the countries in this book are not representative of all the countries in the world, it is obvious that there are both similarities and differences in the dynamics of elder abuse as discussed by chapter authors. With this fact in mind, the concluding chapter in this book will attempt to identify both the unique and common experiences regarding elder abuse within countries represented in this volume. Such an assessment might result in greater understanding of the problem and greater awareness of what can be accomplished in preventing, detecting, and intervening in cases of elder abuse.

This chapter will present some general conclusions about the existence of elder abuse in different countries. No attempt will be

[Haworth co-indexing entry note]: "Common and Unique Themes on Elder Abuse from a World-Wide Perspective." Kosberg, Jordan I., and Juanita L. Garcia. Co-published simultaneously in the *Journal of Elder Abuse & Neglect* (The Haworth Press, Inc.) Vol. 6, No. 3/4, 1995, pp. 183-197; and: *Elder Abuse: International and Cross-Cultural Perspectives* (ed: Jordan I. Kosberg, and Juanita L. Garcia) The Haworth Press, Inc., 1995, pp. 183-197. Multiple copies of this article/chapter may be purchased from The Haworth Document Delivery Center [1-800-3-HAWORTH; 9:00 a.m. - 5:00 p.m. (EST)].

made to identify the particular country from which a description or example is drawn, nor to generalize conclusions to other countries of the world. Such efforts are left for further research on the dynamics of elder abuse in different countries, for cross-national studies, and for longitudinal analyses of the impact of societal changes on the problem of elder abuse which might take place as additional knowledge and data become available.

DEFINITIONS OF THE PROBLEM

Many of the countries acknowledged that elder abuse was a new phenomenon, not adequately defined and not adequately studied. Most of the attention on elder abuse as a social problem has occurred within the past 15 years. Several of the authors questioned whether elder abuse is a new phenomenon or whether there is just an increased awareness of the problem. Most of the authors acknowledged that the definition of elder abuse in their country was heavily influenced by the work done within North America and in Great Britain. Most frequently, they included physical abuse, psychological abuse, neglect, self-destructive behavior, and theft. Physical abuse of the elderly was seen to be the rarest form of abuse in several of the countries.

Some differences were noted, however. In one country, elder abuse did not have a rigid chronological definition, inasmuch as the lower life expectancy of the native population precluded most from entering into advanced age. Self-abuse or neglect was eliminated in a few countries, as elder abuse was defined as the interaction between abused and abuser. Intentionality was entered into the "equation" of abuse and unintentional acts of adversity were not seen to be an apparent example of elder abuse.

In one country there was a distinction made between mistreatment (including financial exploitation, verbal abuse, neglect, and over-medication) and abuse (including physical and psychological adversities, sexual assaults, and theft). Some countries made distinctions between intentional harm (called abuse) and passive harm (which was called neglect and not abuse). Relatedly, a distinction was made between acts of commission and acts of omission with the former being a more serious problem.

One author suggested that fear on the part of the elderly should be included as a type of abuse; that is, fear of being abused was as unfortunate as being abused. The consequences of fear were related to emotional problems, suicide, and health impairments; indeed, the overall quality of one's life. A few of the countries introduced the concept of abandonment into the definition of elder abuse. It was suggested that health care settings and law enforcement agencies were the most familiar with cases of elderly persons abandoned by family members. Neglectful behavior, where it existed, was seen to be not only a result of individual inattention but also a lack of formal organizations and institutions (often governments) to provide adequate services for the elderly and/or surveillance over the care of elderly persons within their own homes or within the dwellings of family members.

Elder abuse was also defined as the absence of quality of care. Countries have unique values, such as for privacy, warmth, harmony, and respect. When these values are circumvented or ignored in the care or treatment of an older person, elder abuse is believed to have occurred. In such a definition, the discrepancy between expected behavior or attitudes toward an older person may be seen to be no less tumultuous than physical abuse or financial misappropriation.

EXTENT OF THE PROBLEM

In much of the research on elder abuse coming from North America and Great Britain, the extent of elder abuse is speculative and believed to be an underestimation. Authors in this book admitted that the problem of elder abuse has not yet been adequately studied to permit a projection of its extent and incidence. Those few studies on abuse which have taken place have generally involved a limited, non-random, service-related sample from which generalizations are inadvisable, excluding the population survey conducted in one European town.

Physical abuse of the elderly was seen to be somewhat rare in several of the countries, perhaps because of the general emphasis on non-aggressive behavior dictated by custom or cultural/religious norms. On the other hand, in some countries, the low status or discrimination of certain groups of elderly could be used to explain, in part, the likelihood of their abuse and the level of social tolerance of such maltreatment toward these older persons. For example, elder abuse might be more prevalent and accepted among the elderly from minority groups or disadvantaged backgrounds or among those elderly having impairments or disabilities. Some authors explained elder abuse as resulting from the decline in the status of the elderly in their country.

MAJOR EXPLANATIONS FOR ELDER ABUSE

The majority of authors expressed the belief that elder abuse increased in the face of industrialization or as a result of economic problems in the country. A few authors admitted that elder abuse had always existed (perhaps a result of general indifference to the plight of or resulting from authoritarian attitudes toward disadvantaged groups). In addition, some mistreatment of the elderly was seen to be acceptable and was not identified as abuse. Frail, dependent, and impoverished elderly would be included in such a grouping of individuals. Elder abuse was seen to follow scientific advances in medicine that have resulted in the growth of the elderly population. Lower mortality rates, coming at a period when for economic reasons social and health services are being curtailed, have resulted in increased demands for family caregiving responsibilities of elderly relatives.

Each country explained the dynamics of elder abuse in different ways. There were, however, three common themes that seemed to permeate the chapters in this book: dependency, economic conditions, and cultural change.

Dependency. It was believed by some authors that dependency of an older person places heavy responsibilities on the shoulders of family caregivers. This, in turn, leads to higher demands for care and greater burdens for caregivers (and elder abuse is one type of consequence). In a situation where family responsibility is a norm, there will be a greater proportion of family members who are caring for a more-impaired population of elderly persons. With greater longevity for more elderly, care will be given for longer periods of time. Thus, more elderly will be dependent upon more family members for longer periods of time; thereby creating a greater probability of elder abuse.

Physical dependency, in contrast to economic and social dependency, was seen to have the strongest relationship to elder abuse. Such needs, for care and attention, placed special requirements on family caregivers. Often such responsibilities were distasteful to those providing care (such as bathing, toileting, and feeding assistance).

Economic Conditions. Many of the authors believed that economic difficulties in countries had direct and indirect influences on the existence of elder abuse. Economic recession in a country can lead to the growing problem of unemployment. Given a reduction in income, family members may seek out the savings, earnings, and property of elderly relatives. The potential for economic exploitation is thus increased. With an underemployed population, crime and violence often increase. Inasmuch as elderly persons, especially the most vulnerable, are often sought out as "easy prey" for utilitarian crime, the chapter authors suggested that elder abuse and victimization of the elderly increased with the increase in economic problems.

Another consequence of national economic recession was seen to be the reduction of programs and services. Given the competition between groups in need, the likely existence of ageism, and a cultural belief in filial responsibility for the care of the elderly, it was felt that resources for the elderly are often the ones to be cut back. Governments respond to periods of economic scarcity by reconsidering the eligibility criteria for public assistance, the forms of assistance to be given, and the level of such assistance. As discussed in the welfare-state countries of this book, cutbacks in the normal provisions to citizens is either taking place or is seriously being considered.

In the past, residents of welfare states did not worry about growing old. But with the decline of the economy (and budget cuts and increased competition between groups) and the increase in the number and proportion of the elderly, attitudes have changed. Further, in the past, institutional care had been used in part for more effective care and for relief of families. Presently, there is an effort to maintain the elderly for as long as possible in the community. This means, in effect, family caregiving will be needed.

Portraying the family as a panacea for the care of the elderly (whether or not desired by the family) can result in resentment, anger, and depression. The possibility is great that the elderly person will be the scapegoat and that abuse will occur. A final consequence of economic problems to a country presented by the authors, including those from the welfare state countries, was the privatization of resources (the development of market-place capitalism). Since the private sector better serves more affluent populations, it was believed that resources for the elderly (which might supplement or replace family assistance) would be available for wealthier individuals. Thus, elder abuse by family members would more likely occur within impoverished families who did not have alternatives available to them for the care they provided to their elderly relatives.

Cultural Changes. Several of the authors believed that elder abuse resulted from rapid changes in tradition/customs regarding respect of the older members of society and in the caregiving responsibilities for the family. The authors from developing nations alluded to the consequences of industrialization and technological advancements in the care of the elderly. Reference was made to the resulting values of individualization, impersonalization, and changing lifestyles. The consequences of such changes, in some instances, did not benefit the role and status of the elderly within the family and in society. Fear by the elderly, in general, was seen to be related not only to crime on the street but also (more currently) within the home as well.

An elderly relative who has maintained traditional expectations for family responsibility might face a conflict with those members of the family (such as children) who hold more Westernized values and who may not wish to take on such caregiving tasks. Anger, resentment, and guilt by family caregivers who take on unwanted responsibilities for an elderly relative might result in abuse of the (dependent) person requiring the care.

Traditional caregivers have always been the female members of the family. Yet, in several of the countries represented in this book, there was a high rate of women working outside the home. The social changes were generally seen to result in a decrease in the stability of family relationships. A related factor is the possible resentment of female caregivers who might be forced to go from full- to part-time employment or leave their jobs and careers due to caregiving needs at home for an elderly relative.

SIGNIFICANT VARIABLES RELATED TO ELDER ABUSE

In addition to the belief that elder abuse was associated with the economic climate, the dependency of older persons on the abusing caregiver, and cultural changes, other variables were also seen as relevant. Chapters in this book reflected a general belief that abused persons were more likely to be women, impoverished, living alone, uneducated, physically or mentally frail, and socially, psychologically, and economically dependent on others. The following are summaries of the common topics that emerged regarding the characteristics of abused and abusing individuals and situations.

Socio-Economic Level. Although economic problems were seen related to elder abuse, it was suggested that high risk elderly can come from more affluent as well as impoverished backgrounds. As has been mentioned, while older persons from lower socioeconomic levels might be more economically dependent (and have family members who also suffer from economic hardships), those from higher socioeconomic levels might be more likely to be taken advantage of financially.

Marital Status. Abuse of elderly women is viewed as a continuation of the cycle of marital violence. This conclusion suggests that spouse abuse extending into old age is considered a form of elder abuse. While in the majority of cases it was the wife who was abused, an abused wife could "turn on" her formerly-abusing husband when he became frail and became dependent upon her. The likelihood of spouse abuse among the elderly was seen to be highly related to the problem drinking of the abuser.

Substance Abuse. A drinking problem was a common explanation for both being abused and being an abuser. Often the excessive drinking by both parties takes place at the same time under the same roof and results in abuse perpetrated by one and an inability of the other to defend himself/herself.

Personal Problems. Authors acknowledged that elder abuse resulted from the actions of family members who were inappropriate caregivers. In addition to being substance abusers, those who might maltreat dependent elderly family members were relatives who had emotional problems, cognitive impairments, or physical limitations. Inasmuch as care could be provided by a spouse, sibling, or adult child of advanced age, the care by such an elderly caregiver could be adversely affected by the consequences of advanced age. Also, formerly dependent children (such as those with mental retardation or emotional problems) might become the caregivers of their increasingly-dependent elderly parents.

Isolation. Given the growth of the old-old segment of the population, there was an increasingly-high proportion of older persons who were not married (who had never married or who were widowed). These older persons tended to be isolated and lonely which, in turn, increased their vulnerability and the possibility of elder abuse. Depression of an older person (related to the quality of life) was seen to result from isolation and a lack of friends.

Gender. Women are more likely to be abused simply because they predominate among elderly persons. Further, it was suggested that women in several of the countries are more likely to have lower levels of educational attainment and thus are more (economically) dependent upon others. In the face of changing norms and values, the traditional role of older women in the home of their children is seen to be undergoing modifications resulting in a reduction of influence and importance. Women are more likely to live with their families and, therefore, more likely to be subjected to family maltreatment. Single older women, living alone, in urban areas were also seen to be especially vulnerable to elder abuse.

Cultural Homogeneity. Countries range in the heterogeneity of their population. For example, the authors of chapters on Scandinavian countries indicated that the populations were rather homogeneous. One could make an assumption that the homogeneity of not only the elderly population, but of national values and characteristics between the elderly and younger members of the society, could well be related to the desire to provide more adequate care and attention (by both the family and society). Sharp distinctions within and between generations in a country (for example, by race), coupled with a history of antagonism and prejudice, might predict adversity for those elderly coming from more powerless groups in the country.

Housing. The shortage of housing resources for all citizens was translated into the need for multigenerational households. In cases when such arrangements were not desired or resulted in overcrowding, vulnerable older members of the family were more likely to become victims of abuse. With the absence of suitable housing facilities for the elderly, the older members of society often had no recourse but to live (albeit, grudgingly) in the dwellings of their younger family members. The alternative of living with family members or living in age-segregated housing for the elderly is for the older person to live alone. This, in turn, was seen related to loneliness, poverty, anger, alcoholism, and addiction to medications.

Societal Violence. Elder abuse was seen by some to be related to the extent to which aggression, violence, and lawlessness was present in the general society. An assumption raised by such a conjecture, which has yet to be empirically-tested, is that the more law abiding a society is, the less likely the rates of elder abuse. As had been mentioned, crime rates seem related to the economic conditions in a country. Thus, there is an interrelationship between economic conditions, crime and violence, and elder abuse.

EFFORTS TO COMBAT THE PROBLEM

The authors of chapters concluded that before a country can identify the causes of elder abuse, there are several prerequisites which need to be addressed. First of all, there must be an awareness of the problem of elder abuse. There must be an understanding of the dynamics which cause the problem and a commitment to resolve the problem. Several of the authors cautioned that there might be resistance to combating the problem of elder abuse which arises out of prevalent societal values. Strong among such cultural "roadblocks" are family privacy, reluctance to publicize personal, family, and social problems to outsiders, respect for the head of the household, and family traditions. Despite this caveat, the chapters in this book did identify many methods by which elderly abuse was addressed and abused individuals given assistance.

General Efforts. Some countries did not differentiate victims of crime or abuse by age, and the elderly were included in the general efforts (for crime detection and prevention) for any victim in the country. For example, in some countries there were general efforts made to protect helpless or dependent persons of any age. So, too, were the elderly a concern (along with all others) of coalition formations focusing upon crime, victims rights, intrafamily abuse, and violence. Some authors did admit, however, that it was necessary to ensure that the elderly, in general, and elder abuse, in particular, were not forgotten in education, training, and intervention efforts that had general non-specific emphases.

Verifying the Problem. The specific national focus on elder abuse was seen to necessitate the substantiation of the problem. While impressionistic accounts, headlines in newspapers, or case studies by practitioners, policymakers, and program planners were viewed to have some impact on the identification of elder abuse, more systematic and rigorous reporting was believed to be necessary. To achieve the goal of empirical verification of elder abuse in a country, apart from methodological and conceptual difficulties in the definition and measurement, there is the difficulty in getting abused persons to admit to others that they suffer adversity at the hands of relatives (i.e., sons and daughters). The conspiracy of "family silence" can take place along with the fear that the solution to one's problem (of abuse) is greater than the problem. This is to suggest that often the elderly victims of abuse assume that, if their problem is detected, removal from their home and institutionalization will result, a consequence many are not prepared to accept.

Also related to the collection of data on elder abuse is the perceived reliability of reports of abuse coming from older persons. It has been suggested that accuracy of reporting (cognitive ability) of an older person may be in question. Further, as a family problem, it is often very difficult (if not impossible) to corroborate the contentions made by an older person.

Given the knowledge that elder abuse exists, the dynamics are understood, the commitment to do something about the problem is made, and the extent of the problem is substantiated, efforts should be undertaken to develop treatment and prevention programs.

Social Support for Families. Several of the authors stressed the need of family caregivers for supportive services. Support for such assistance was seen to come from governmental sources. Inasmuch as elder abuse was thought to result from the frustrations and burdens of over-worked caregivers, respite care was believed to be a high priority for family caregivers. It was viewed as a vital preventive program for caregivers who were under extreme duress as a result of caregiving demands by impaired elderly persons.

Alternatives to Family Care. For those elderly who either had no family members to provide care for them or for those families which could not or should not provide such care, alternatives to family caregiving was discussed. Such alternatives pertain to efforts at maintaining elder persons living independently in the community (through programs and services provided to them within their dwellings) as well as through the creation of alternatives to living in the home of family members. Such needed resources include housing for the elderly, foster care, and group-living facilities.

Family Life Education and Counseling. Some authors alluded to the need to provide families which guidance, counseling, and encouragement in their efforts at caregiving for impaired elderly relatives. It was believed to be important that family members who are experiencing mounting pressures and tensions in their caregiving roles seek out professional guidance prior to the potential development of an abusing situation. Such a plan requires general community awareness and education about elder abuse along with community services that provide counseling and guidance for caregivers of the elderly.

Support Groups for Family Caregivers. In an increasing number of countries there are support groups for individuals who have similar problems (i.e., substance abuse, mental and physical illnesses) and their family members. While it is still uncommon to have support groups for abused older persons (although there are such groups for child and spouse abuse victims), there are those who would advocate for such groups. Far more common are support groups for those who care for impaired older individuals (with Alzheimer's disease or terminal illness). The peer support and professional guidance received in such groups can be beneficial to a caregiver in verbalizing frustrations and in receiving suggestions for dealing with mounting pressures and demands. Clearly, in doing so, the likelihood that elder abuse will result from the burdens is diminished.

Detection Protocols. Since elder abuse is difficult to identify, there was some discussion about the need to implement detection protocols to be used in the identification of elder abuse. Generally, such screening instruments were seen to be necessary for use within health care settings.

Advocacy. Most of the authors urged the formation of advocacy groups and advocacy efforts in combating the problem of elder abuse. Government was seen to play a leadership role in such efforts. However, wide-spread public efforts to prevent and intervene in the problem of elder abuse would necessitate financial resources and governmental action.

Public Policies. The majority of countries represented in this book did not have policies that focused specifically on elder abuse; the elderly were included in policies that protected individuals of all ages. In this regard, it was deemed important to determine if, in fact, the elderly are covered to the same extent as younger persons. In some countries, elderly persons were covered in policy provisions for specific problems. For example, in one country, policies for the vulnerable elderly were incorporated in legislation for the mentally ill. However, it was felt that elderly persons (regardless of their physical or mental condition) were unfairly stigmatized by being included in legislation for psychiatric populations. Further, subsuming attention for elder abuse within a mental health structure was seen to possibly stop some elderly persons from seeking assistance.

Social security policies were lacking in some countries which precluded their elderly citizens from the opportunity for self-determination and independence. Also, policies were needed to create more hospitals, centers for the aged, guest houses, and other resources. There was also a need discussed for more comprehensive community care systems and for a coordinating mechanism to ensure the effectiveness of such a system of community resources.

Public policies which specifically focus on the problem of elderly abuse were discussed by the authors. For example, a telephone helpline for abused individuals and for stressed caregivers was advocated by one author. Another believed that professionals should have a mandated responsibility to report cases of elder abuse that came to their attention. No formal Adult Protective Service program which would provide surveillance over and assistance for the most vulnerable elderly individuals existed in any of the countries.

Housing Resources. Appeals for additional housing resources for the elderly emerged in several chapters. Such an increase in dwellings would alleviate over-crowding resulting from the need of elderly relatives to live with their families. So too housing for the elderly would create an opportunity for independence and an alternative for having to live with family members and in institutional placements. The need to be cautious about creating incentives for intergenerational living was mentioned. Such economic encouragement, it was suggested, might create the wrong incentive for wanting to live with elderly relatives.

Action by Elderly Persons. Consistent with other efforts by disadvantaged and victimized groups, it was recommended that the elderly, themselves, engage in group efforts to combat those conditions related to the existence of elder abuse (as well as a frontal attack on the problem itself). In many of the countries represented in this book, the elderly were beginning to organize themselves and to take on advocacy efforts. Led by the elderly (often through their organizations), coordinated activities could bring together the elderly and lay and professional members of the community to engage in advocacy for the problem of elder abuse.

Publicity. The need for wide-spread publicity on the problem of elder abuse was stressed by many of the authors. For action to take place, the social problem needs to be widely recognized as a problem. The need for public initiatives to combat the problem was stressed. One method suggested to achieve this goal was to heighten both public and political awareness. Much can be accomplished by using the mass media, films, books, and magazines, to bring the reality of elder abuse to the citizens in every country. Relatedly, of course, is publicizing the problem to those in the helping professions. This is best accomplished through the formal education of future employees and through inservice and staff development efforts of current employees within social and health care systems. Changes in attitudes toward the elderly are needed. There seemed to be a general lack of education about aging and old age, a deficit that appeared to be related to the lack of awareness of elder abuse and the resources to do anything about it.

CONCLUDING THOUGHTS

Tradition and modernization are at a cross-road in many countries of the world (as represented by the chapters in this text). The customs of care of and respect for the elderly are strained as a result of social and demographic changes. One result of this conflict between the traditional ways and contemporary values and behaviors is elder abuse.

The information that is contained within each chapter is a reflection of the availability of knowledge (both conceptual and empirical) within a particular time period and the backgrounds and perspectives of the authors. Accordingly, with time, it is suspected that more will be known and written about the dynamics of elder abuse in different countries of the world. It is hoped that with increased attention to the problem of elder abuse, program planners and policy-makers will become more knowledgeable and more resources will be available for the elderly and their caregivers.

As mentioned by the contributing authors, elder abuse exists and it will not quickly nor easily disappear. In fact, the problem will probably increase as a worldwide social problem. Countries are aging; the number and proportion of the elderly are increasing, especially the oldest of the old. It is this group of elderly who demand the most in way of care and attention by families. It is this group who will probably be the most vulnerable to abusive behavior. As was also noted in this book, economic problems, changing values, and general lawlessness contribute to the existence of elder abuse. Until and unless these characteristics of contemporary societies are challenged and improved, efforts at combating elder abuse can only be, at best, partially effective.

The work on elder abuse coming from the U.S., Canada, and Great Britain is now joined by a growing volume of literature emanating from other countries. This information on elder abuse needs to be synthesized and analyzed. Out of such efforts should arise a better understanding of the causes and consequences of elder abuse, the contribution of culture, and useful suggestions for the prevention and detection of the problem, and for program and policy initiatives for effective intervention efforts.

It is hoped that this book of readings on elder abuse as it occurs in but a few countries in the world may be a step toward international dialogue and analysis. Elder abuse is a social problem that affects all of us personally, if not professionally, as caring members of society.

Index

Note: Page numbers followed by f indicate figures; those followed by t indicate tables.

   199

Haworth
DOCUMENT DELIVERY
SERVICE

This new service provides a single-article order form for any article from a Haworth journal.

- *Time Saving:* No running around from library to library to find a specific article.
- *Cost Effective:* All costs are kept down to a minimum.
- *Fast Delivery:* Choose from several options, including same-day FAX.
- *No Copyright Hassles:* You will be supplied by the original publisher.
- *Easy Payment:* Choose from several easy payment methods.

Open Accounts Welcome for . . .
- Library Interlibrary Loan Departments
- Library Network/Consortia Wishing to Provide Single-Article Services
- Indexing/Abstracting Services with Single Article Provision Services
- Document Provision Brokers and Freelance Information Service Providers

MAIL or *FAX* THIS ENTIRE ORDER FORM TO:

Haworth Document Delivery Service
The Haworth Press, Inc.
10 Alice Street
Binghamton, NY 13904-1580

or FAX: (607) 722-6362
or CALL: 1-800-3-HAWORTH
(1-800-342-9678; 9am-5pm EST)

PLEASE SEND ME PHOTOCOPIES OF THE FOLLOWING SINGLE ARTICLES:

1) Journal Title: _____
   Vol/Issue/Year:_____Starting & Ending Pages:_____
   Article Title:_____
   _____

2) Journal Title: _____
   Vol/Issue/Year:_____Starting & Ending Pages:_____
   Article Title:_____
   _____

3) Journal Title: _____
   Vol/Issue/Year:_____Starting & Ending Pages:_____
   Article Title:_____
   _____

4) Journal Title: _____
   Vol/Issue/Year:_____Starting & Ending Pages:_____
   Article Title:_____
   _____

(See other side for Costs and Payment Information)

COSTS: Please figure your cost to order quality copies of an article.

1. Set-up charge per article: $8.00

        ($8.00 × number of separate articles)   _____

2. Photocopying charge for each article:

        1-10 pages: $1.00   _____

        11-19 pages: $3.00   _____

        20-29 pages: $5.00   _____

        30+ pages: $2.00/10 pages   _____

3. Flexicover (optional): $2.00/article   _____

4. Postage & Handling: US: $1.00 for the first article/

        $.50 each additional article   _____

        Federal Express: $25.00   _____

        Outside US: $2.00 for first article/

        $.50 each additional article _____

5. Same-day FAX service: $.35 per page   _____

                    GRAND TOTAL: _____

METHOD OF PAYMENT: (please check one)

❑ Check enclosed   ❑ Please ship and bill. PO # _____

        (sorry we can ship and bill to bookstores only! All others must pre-pay)

❑ Charge to my credit card: ❑ Visa; ❑ MasterCard; ❑ American Express;

Account Number: _____ Expiration date: _____

Signature: *X*_____

Name: _____ Institution: _____

Address: _____

_____

City: _____ State: _____ Zip: _____

Phone Number: _____ FAX Number: _____

MAIL or *FAX* THIS ENTIRE ORDER FORM TO:

Haworth Document Delivery Service	**or FAX:** (607) 722-6362
The Haworth Press, Inc.	**or CALL:** 1-800-3-HAWORTH
10 Alice Street	(1-800-342-9678; 9am-5pm EST)
Binghamton, NY 13904-1580	